Designing Instructional Swim Programs

for Individuals with Disabilities

Marcia Jean Carter

Mary A. Dolan

Stephen P. LeConey

Photographs by Cincinnati Recreation Commission, Therapeutic Recreation Division and Northern Suburban Special Recreation Association of Northfield, Illinois

D1708027

Sponsored by the

American Association for Leisure and Recreation

an association of the

American Alliance for Health, Physical Education,

Recreation and Dance

The American Alliance for Health, Physical Education, Recreation and Dance is an educational organization designed to support, encourage, and provide assistance to member groups and their personnel nationwide as they initiate, develop, and conduct programs in health, leisure, and movement-related activities. The Alliance seeks to:

- Encourage, guide, and support professional growth and development in health, leisure, and movement-related programs based on individual needs, interests, and capabilities.
- Communicate the importance of health, leisure, and movement-related activities as they contribute to human well-being.
- Encourage and facilitate research which will enrich health, leisure, and movement-related activities and to disseminate the findings to professionals and the public.
- Develop and evaluate standards and guidelines for personnel and programs in health, leisure, and movement-related activities.
- Coordinate and administer a planned program of professional, public, and government relations that will improve education in areas of health, leisure, and movement-related activities.
- Conduct other activities for the public benefit.

Front cover: Individual with Down syndrome develops propulsion skills.
Back cover, top: Adults find both social and physical benefits with aquatic experiences. Middle: Swimmer with autism acquires skills in deep water with instructor encouragement. Bottom: Goggles facilitate water adjustment for many individuals.

ISBN 0-88314-559-6

Contents

About the Authors

Marcia Jean Carter, Re.D. CLP, CTRS, is Director of Leisure Services, School of Education, Department of Health, Human Performance & Recreation, Baylor University, Waco, Texas,

Mary A. Dolan is Aquatic Director in the Therapeutic Recreation Division of the Cincinnati Recreation Commission, Cincinnati, Ohio.

Stephen P. LeConey, M.S., CTRS, is Supervisor, Therapeutic Recreation Division, Cincinnati Recreation Commission, Cincinnati, Ohio.

Organization

This manual is prepared as a resource to complement existing established aquatic programs (Red Cross, YMCA). The material might be used to supplement swim instructor certification programs, since adapted aquatics instructor credentials are no longer available. The content also provides users with information on accommodations required by the Americans with Disabilities Act (ADA).

An instructional swimming progression applicable to children and adults with disabilities is presented. Teaching strategies described in the swimming progression enable staff in community and clinical aquatic settings to make their programs more accessible and inclusionary to individuals with disabilities as required by ADA. Focus is placed first on the instructional progression and second on the modification of the progression as it might be used with individuals having various disabilities.

Content and methods of the manual have been field tested on persons with various disabilities by instructors holding adapted aquatics certificates (no longer available). Material is supplemented by information from recognized aquatic resources and experts in therapeutic-recreation.

The manual begins with an introduction that briefly covers philosophy, necessary definitions, and a theoretical model. Sample forms to use in recording progress and outcomes appear in the Appendix. Community aquatic personnel might use the forms and principles drawn from the philosophy and model to plan services that would make their waterfront areas and programs more accessible and have a greater appeal to all community residents. The programming approach and presented resources ;might be used to enhance existing or design new aquatic services to accommodate persons with or without temporary or permanent illnesses and disabilities.

The bulk of the manual is arranged as follows:

The swim progression and specific instructional techniques as well as assessment and teaching suggestions are detailed in the first section. Swimmer behavior management procedures and a swim lesson plan form to use in the actual delivery of daily programs are presented.

In the second section, swimming with individuals having various disabilities is presented. Material reviews population descriptors, aquatic precautions, and practical applications useful during instruction.

Management tasks are outlined in the next section. Factors considered include personnel, safety in the aquatic environment, management of the instructional setting, and accessibility of the setting and instructional resources. Resources available are noted as well as devices personnel may craft to individualize instruction with each participant. When implemented, the identified adaptations support the intent of ADA.

Concluding the manual are a glossary, list of associations, reference list, sample recording forms, and index. The sources listed were used in the preparation of this manual and offer the reader access to sources useful in aquatic programs with individuals with disabilities.

Throughout the manual, exhibits and photos of actual experiences are incorporated to enhance and clarify the text.

Introduction

In 1990, a major piece of legislation, the Americans with Disabilities Act (ADA), shifted the focus from "adapted" or "segregated" programs to aquatic opportunities that include individuals with disabilities. Henceforth, "adapting the aquatic experience" becomes the responsibility of anyone associated with an aquatic facility whether it be the aquatics program director, lifeguard, or swim class instructor. Thus, familiarity with the purposes of ADA becomes a necessity.

The Americans with Disabilities Act was signed into law by President George Bush on July 26, 1990. The act has been called the "Bill of Rights for People with Disabilities" as it guarantees access to every critical service and area of life. An individual with a disability is defined as one who:

> Has a physical or mental impairment that substantially limits one or more of the major life
> activities of that individual, or has a record of such an impairment, or is regarded as having such
> an impairment (McGovern, 1992).

This definition only excludes those who are currently illegally abusing substances and are homosexual or bisexual. "Major life activity" includes recreation, education, work, mobility, transportation, and communication. Local government provisions are defined in Title II, Public Services, which requires that programs and services must be made equally accessible to persons with disabilities. Services including recreation are to be made available in settings where participants do not have disabilities, the least restrictive environment.

Further, the law requires three types of reasonable modification to accommodate the disability of an otherwise qualified individual:

1. Rules, policies, and practices of the agency: Modification of, for example, registration procedures or other policies that might limit participation.

2. Removal of architectural, transportation, or communication barriers: Installation of telecommunication devices, elimination of architectural barriers, and provision of accessible vehicles.

3. Provision of auxiliary aids or services: Use of a sign interpreter or additional staff to provide assistance to persons with mental or physical disabilities.

These accommodations suggest more than physical accessibility. The law requires program accessibility. Thus, access to aquatic experiences is considered with instructional modifications, staff training, lifeguard preparation, pool rules, safety and risk management plans, classes offered, enrollment and registration procedures, and the use of modified equipment.

Aquatic programs provided in the community through government funded agencies like public or special leisure service districts, by law, must accommodate persons with disabilities. ADA implies that inclusionary opportunities are most appropriate with services provided by any agency. Swimming by its very nature is an "inclusionary experience." Skill parity is not essential to enjoy the experience with others, nor is age. It is a leisure experience which may be enjoyed by all in a variety of aquatic settings including wave pools and water parks. Becoming safe in the water fosters participation in boating, fishing, sailing, and water skiing. Swimming brings families together. Skills acquired during supervised swim instruction enhance behaviors in other areas like independent living and functional academics.

Program Philosophy

Therapeutic recreation uses a variety of modalities to affect participant health and well-being. The physical properties of water contribute to its use as a modality having psychological, sociological, and physiological benefits. Awareness of these properties and their potential impact on the swimmer enables the instructor to individualize the experience to accommodate participants with various disabilities. Of the properties presented, buoyancy is perhaps the most significant. As a result of buoyancy, persons with physical impairments experience freedom of movement in the water not found on land.

Buoyancy: A total or partial immersion in water that results in an upward thrust and a degree of weightlessness. Buoyancy enables increased mobility while, to some extent, negatively impacting balance: To illustrate, a person who can not achieve independent mobility on land may move independently in the water; while a person who is able to maintain a standing balance on land may experience difficulty in the water.

Density/Relative Density: Buoyancy is influenced by density. Relative density of water is 1. Objects less dense than water will float; objects more dense will sink quickly; and objects equally as dense as water will float just below the surface. With the lungs inflated, relative density of the human body is .95 to .97; without the lungs inflated, relative density of the human body is 1.05 to 1.08. We expel air from the lungs to immerse ourselves in water; and, conversely, we inhale to remain buoyant. Thus, the ability to inflate/deflate the lungs affects the ability to float.

Viscosity: A form of friction created by the molecules in a substance. Viscosity acts as a resistance to movement as the molecules of a liquid tend to adhere to the surface of a body moving through it. Air has less viscosity than water; therefore, a body moving through air encounters less resistance than a body moving through water. Thus, the larger the object moving through the water, the more resistance it encounters. This resistance is used, for example, to increase muscle tone and strength.

Surface Tension: A cohesion is created by the attraction between neighboring molecules of the same type of matter (water) as they encounter molecules of a different type of matter (air and/or human body): This tension manifests itself as an elastic skin at the surface of the water. As a consequence, there is greater resistance to movement at the water's surface than there is beneath the surface level; thus, to swim below the water is actually easier than to swim at the water's surface. The aquatic environment possesses several qualities that have an effect on participant functioning. The therapeutic recreation process of assessment, planning, implementation, and evaluation is used to design and deliver aquatic programs. During this process, participants' skill levels are determined via needs assessment. Then experiences are planned to affect swimming skills and cognitive, affective, social, and emotional functioning. Participants are placed in aquatic programs which best address their assessed needs and result in enhanced swimming skills and personal well-being.

Refraction: As a light ray moves from a more dense to a less dense medium it bends. Refraction affects a swimmer's estimation of depth perception. This effect is seen as persons judge distances from above the water to the pool floor or lake bottom since the density of the air and the water vary.

The therapeutic recreation process of assessment, planning, implementation, and evaluation is used to design and deliver aquatic programs. During this process, participants' skill levels are determined via needs assessment. Then experiences are planned to affect swimming skills and cognitive, affective, social, and emotinal functioning. Participants are placed in aquatic programs which best address their assessed needs and result in enhanced swimming skills and personal well-being.

One programming approach organizes aquatic services along a participant skill continuum that has inclusion as an ultimate goal, the intent of the ADA legislation. This approach recognizes that specific participation outcomes are influenced by participant functioning capacity, and that the degree of staff intervention is dependent upon participant functioning level.

Individual attention is given to assessed needs of each participant.

Levels on this skill continuum are defined as follows: Participants in Skill Level I programs benefit from recreation therapy interventions designed to improve functional skills like range of motion, ambulation, and emotional tolerance. Persons in cardiac rehabilitation programs represent those who might participate in Level I aquatics. Participants in Skill Level II, adapted or specialized aquatics, have disabilities that affect their acquisition and use of aquatic skills. To illustrate, persons with cognitive impairments might be unable to manage their self-care needs while persons with physical impairments might require assistance learning how to access aquatic facilities. Skill Level II programs have as outcomes not only aquatic skill development but also those rehabilitative and educational experiences supplementary to aquatics yet essential in the mainstream.

Participants in Skill Level III, mainstream and integrative programs, possess the social skills and are capable of acquiring aquatic skills for use in mainstreamed settings; what is lacking is exposure to and training in mainstreamed settings. Skill Level III classes are also intended to support prior skill acquisition. Some persons may choose to remain in these programs because instruction is necessary to retain their skill levels and security and companionship result

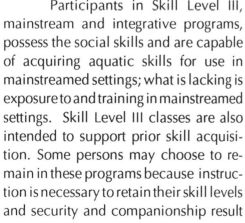

Inclusionary programs are the responsibility of all aquatic staff.

from familiar faces and places. Skill Level IV or LINK (Leisure Integration Network) is inclusionary programs with staff serving as resource trainers and facilitators. These aquatic programs are individualized to neighborhood pools and aquatic centers which participants regularly frequent.

This service continuum guides the staff planning process. Staffing and resources are allocated accordingly. To illustrate, the staff to participant ratio, water temperature and depth, and assistive devices used during each session are prescribed by skill level. This continuum also serves as a self-assessment screening and placement tool with program participants. Prior to program entry and as participants complete their annual information form (pertinent medical and behavioral data), they review and select skill level classes suited to their functional abilities and aquatic needs.

A supplemental aquatic registration form requests information about participants' capabilities to manage themselves in and around the water and to respond to and participate in instructional classes. To illustrate, ability to dress, ambulate to and from the pool, and to see and hear the instructor are elements assessed. Together, the annual information form and aquatic registration form serve as initial assessments and are used by staff to confirm selected classes or recommend placement in classes at an alternative skill level. The assessment process is actually completed during initial class sessions when staff observe swimmers to affirm aquatic skill levels and general functioning ability. With this information, staff write individual participant aquatic objectives that guide their intervention.

Writing of individual objectives is the initial step in planning of the intervention. A second planning step is to identify at what point along the swimming skill sequence to commence instruction. This is determined by comparing the participant's abilities to the task-analyzed steps in the swimming progression, then placing the swimmer in a class where instruction covers previously unmastered skills.

Classes, implementation of the service, are organized to recognize a swimming progression. Participants receive instruction intended to move them along a sequenced skill progression to the next higher skill levels. The evaluation step of the therapeutic recreation process occurs as the staff ascertain the participant's progress along the continuum as compared to a swimmer's objectives. Consequently, these objectives along with pertinent assessment data are computerized and retained by staff as classes are conducted. These forms are updated with each program cycle to reflect participant progress and capture new assessment information used to confirm program placements and/or recommend alternatives suited to a swimmer's abilities.

Additional staff assist persons with various disabilities to access aquatic experiences.

Leisure Service Descriptors

Level   **Functional Ability**

I   Persons whose personal needs, instruction, and activity participation are enhanced by individualized assistance. Deficits are evident in self-help, communication, social, emotional, motor, cognitive, and aquatic skills. Staff to participant ratio, for safety and instruction, is one to one or two.

II   Persons function in groups and with minimal assistance communicate and manage personal needs. Gross motor and limited self-help skills are displayed. Focus is on refinement of fine motor skills like stroke coordination and breathing, development of relevant social/emotional skills, and enhancement of self-help skills. Staff to participant ratio is one to four (approximately).

III   Persons manage and communicate their needs and have developed fundamental motor and social interaction skills. Persons lack experience in integrative opportunities, feel secure in their present environment, and require practice to promote skill retention. Youth with chronic disabilities and adults with strokes may prefer these programs. Usual staff to participant ratio is one to eight (or more).

LINK   Leisure Integration Network. With specialized instruction and/or assistance persons develop skill levels adequate to ensure success during integrative experiences. Individualized aquatic instruction is provided in neighborhood and community pools regularly frequented by the participant.

Level I therapy program in cardiac rehabilitation.

Level II adapted program develops stroke coordination.

Level III mainstream program develops social skills.

Aquatic Service Descriptors

Therapeutic programs

Therapy-oriented programs conducted in the water by highly qualified aquatic personnel, certified therapeutic recreation specialists, and physical or occupational therapists, as prescribed by the treatment or rehabilitation plan. Focus is on functional skill improvement rather than "learning to swim." Persons assessed as Level I participate in therapeutic programs.

Specific objectives include:
- Improve range of motion
- Improve strength of trunk and/or extremities
- Improve sitting or standing balance
- Reduce muscle contraction
- Improve ambulation
- Improve cardiovascular endurance
- Improve respiratory function
- Improve cognitive functioning, such as problem solving
- Improve posture
- Improve body awareness
- Improve perceptual and spatial awareness

Adapted/specialized programs

Instructional methods and interactions with persons are modified to ensure skill acquisition and personal development. Becoming water safe, developing a leisure skill, and learning to swim are primary objectives. Concomitant skills address support areas such as dressing and ambulation necessary to access swimming experiences. Persons assessed as Level II and III participate in adapted aquatic programs.

Specific objectives include:
- Develop and improve swim skills
- Develop and improve water and personal safety skills
- Improve self-care skills related to swimming, such as dressing
- Improve independence like water entry-exit and ambulation
- Increase social interaction skills
- Improve self-concept

Mainstream/integrative programs

Persons who are assessed as either having or being capable of developing social skills necessary to group experiences participate in either individualized instruction or group instruction in integrated settings like neighborhood pools. Objectives are either to develop advanced swim skills or to learn to swim in a normalized setting with secondary foci on peer interactions and public behavior development.

Specific objectives include:
- Develop age-appropriate social interaction skills
- Develop fitness and physical well-being
- Develop community resource awareness and access
- Create awareness by the community-at-large of swimming abilities of persons with impairments
- Develop friendships among swimmers with and without disabilities

Theoretical Model

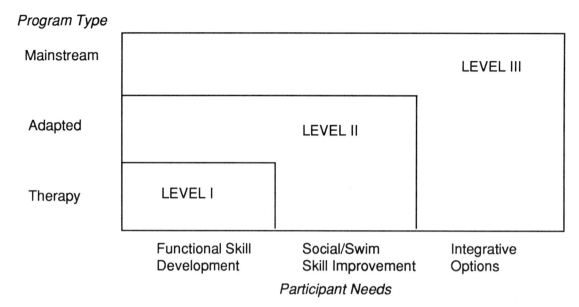

Program Type

Mainstream			LEVEL III
Adapted		LEVEL II	
Therapy	LEVEL I		
	Functional Skill Development	Social/Swim Skill Improvement	Integrative Options

Participant Needs

Service Level Parameters

Program Parameters	Level I	Level II	Level III
Assessment information	Complete medical workup	Specific medical and behavioral concerns	Some medical and history of aquatic experiences
Water temperature	90 to 92	88 to 90	86-88
Ratio	One to one/two	One to three/ four or one to one for beg.	One to eight or more
*Staff	CTRS	Qualified swim instructor with training and experience	Qualified instructor with training
Pool depth	4 to 5 ft for major portion/entire	Shallow portion with full range of depths	Standard depths
Personal assistance	Full physical assistance with dressing and pool entry/exit	Partial physical assistance with dressing and pool entry/exit	Upon request
Assistive equipment	Accessibility aids, dressing tables, and teaching devices	Adapted instructional devices	Personal aquatic aids

*Qualified lifeguard present at all times with all participants

Swim Progression and Instructional Techniques

This section of the manual focuses on the actual instruction and management of participants in the aquatic setting. The opening paragraphs review each of the four phases of the swim progression. An aquatic assessment is presented, followed by the progression of task-analyzed swim skills. This progression has evolved from field-testing and implementation with persons having a variety of functioning abilities and clinical syndromes. Implementation has occurred in segregated as well as integrated indoor and outdoor settings and during both individual and group lessons.

The next portion contains specific teaching suggestions, which can assist as lessons are prepared and presented and also can assess teaching and intervention effectiveness. Included with the instructional techniques are procedures found effective with participants who exhibit particular characteristics, such as gravitational insecurity, "earthboundness," or hemiplegia. An example form used to organize, present, and evaluate a session is shown. This document serves as a formative evaluation and risk management tool as staff and participant responses and environmental contingencies are recorded.

The closing portion of this section contains behavior management information. This is presented because persons with whom the progression is used exhibit behaviors that impinge on their ability to either develop and/or progress in their acquisition of swim skills. Factors that influence the participant's ability to learn include: characteristics associated with a disability like ability to receive (hear/see) and/or process information (cognitive deficits); secondary or side effects of medication; treatment/rehabilitation plan management strategies; degree of exposure to inclusionary aquatic opportunities; and the expectations and perceptions of those in the aquatic environment.

SWIM PROGRESSION PHASES

The ability to individualize swim instruction is fundamental to successful programs. A decision to individualize is based on assessment data that reveal participants' functioning abilities are not likely to result in achieving the objectives of standard programs. As a consequence, aquatic experiences are adapted to enable achievement of individualized objectives.

Methods utilized in standard progressions, Red Cross and YMCA, provide the basis from which adaptations are made. A fundamental principle is to minimize adaptations after standard methods are attempted. The processes of activity and task analyses guide adaptation. Activity analysis determines the physical skills needed to swim as well as the social, emotional, and cognitive functions used in an aquatic setting like water entry and exit, personal care, and safety. A task analysis of a skill results in a sequence from the first to the last step to be performed to master a skill.

The swim progression incorporates assessment and evaluation into the skill development process. The progression is a blueprint for skill development and the instructor's lesson plans. Skills are arranged in a developmental order or a sequence of prerequisite skills. Instruction commences at the level at which the swimmer is no longer capable of performing the skill; when the swimmer is comfortable with that skill,

Left: Swimmer uses bar bell in deep water to increase leg strength. Use of a skill progression ensures that progress is toward stated objectives.

Below: The first area of development is adjustment to the aquatic environment. The participant needs to be comfortable in the water.

Success in one phase of skill progression is prerequisite to the next. As participant works toward final phase of basic swim stroke competence, a floatation device enhances propulsion in prone glide position.

the next task in the sequence is experienced. Thus, the progression assesses entry level skills and evaluates outcome performances.

The skill progression ensures that progress is toward stated objectives. When progress occurs over a long period of time, as might occur with persons with disabilities, this record is critical. If progress is not apparent, a skill is further analyzed into more precise steps and instruction commences at the proper level. As presented, the swim progression is not a "new" approach but rather a more precise method of presenting fundamental skills so they are individualized to ensure participant success.

In addition to an understanding of fundamental aquatic skills, knowledge of impairments caused by various illnesses and disabilities and an understanding of the physical properties of water are essential. Illness and disability affect performance in and around the water while the properties of water either minimize or compound illness and disability effects. During each step in the progression, the instructor recognizes that interactions among these variables influence outcomes.

Outcomes of the aquatic experience are organized into four phases: adjustment to the aquatic environment, breath control, buoyancy and floatation, and propulsion leading to basic swim strokes. Success in one phase is a prerequisite to the next, yet during a session the instructor may incorporate learning experiences in each of the four areas as teaching strategies and formative assessment techniques. Skills are sequenced for individuals who are ambulatory and nonambulatory. Each step in the sequence becomes an objective. To reach the objective, staff individualize teaching processes after considering the implications of the impairments and the impacts of the water properties on each swimmer.

Adjustment to the Aquatic Environment

Adjustment to the aquatic environment is the first and most important area of development, as it sets the stage for further skill development. The primary outcome of this area is participant comfort in and around the water. The instructor completes a final assessment of functional skills, establishes a communication process, alleviates fear, identifies a comfortable working position for the swimmer in the water, facilitates social and emotional adjustment in and out of the water, ensures control of incontinence, and helps the participant with the use of goggles if necessary.

This adjustment is accomplished with movement exploration, stunts, games, and water exercises. The instructor uses the child's imagination to relate the swim skills to themes or concepts with which they are familiar; teaching techniques have names children recognize, like "superman" float. With adults, comparisons are made to objects with which they are familiar, like rafts or boats that displace water due to additional weight.

Adjustment to the aquatic environment begins as the facility is entered. Sounds, smells, sights, and people may confuse or frighten participants because the experience is new or it reminds participants of uncomfortable past experiences. Signs of fear and reluctance like muscle tension or movement away from the area or an instructor are observed to assess readiness. A calm, firm verbal and physical approach, sprinkling water over the participant's body, is used to encourage actual water entry. Practice in the changing area and actual water entry-exit without others present also is helpful. The participant is encouraged by emphasizing how comfortable and free the swimmer feels in the water. Additional time is allowed to accommodate entry so the participant perceives that entry results from personal initiative rather than the instructor's.

A primary goal of water adjustment is to eliminate fear.

Left: Instruction occurs in chest deep water, with maximum balance.

Right: Bobbing develops breath control.

A desirable working position is at a depth of the participant's chest/sternum. Maximum balance is achieved at this depth; more or less depth affects buoyancy, and if instructor support is used strain is placed on the back and arm muscles. With small children, persons without limb sensation or control, those with spina bifida or spinal cord injury, persons with circulatory problems, and those who are not ambulatory, support is provided by an instructor(s) and comfort in vertical and/or horizontal body position is established.

Once a working position is established, focus is on submerging body parts and retrieving objects to gain comfort with having water cover various body parts, especially the mouth, nose, ears, eyes and head. Depth perception, spacial awareness, and directionality are necessary perceptual motor skills affected by the properties of water. Seeing underwater or feeling the bottom is also a means of overcoming fear of the unknown. Safety is gained with coordination and a knowledge of one's position in relation to other objects and persons in the environment. Adjustment to the entire area's depth, breadth, content, and sensations is planned with each participant.

Breath Control

No other skill is as critical to water safety as the ability to submerge without taking in water. When the water pressure outside the mouth and nose is greater than the pressure of the air inside, water is taken in unless the mouth and nose are closed off or the exhalation force is greater. This requires substantial lung capacity and might be difficult for persons with weak respiratory muscles, like those with muscular dystrophy, heart conditions, cerebral palsy, spinal cord injuries, and speech impairments. In these situations, focus is placed on closing off the mouth and nose so water does not enter.

The most effective method used to develop breath control is through bobbing. A swimmer inhales above the water, then submerges to exhale below the water. Continuous repetitions result in rhythmic breathing as required to swim successfully in a prone position. Another desirable skill is to practice opening the eyes underwater as breathing occurs. Blowing bubbles is a useful teaching technique with swimmers, especially those who can neither open their eyes nor see. When the instructor blows bubbles on participants' hands or other body parts, they feel the air pressure or force of exhalation. Also when the instructor pinches participants' noses, water is less likely to be inhaled and this helps participants establish a breathing pattern. Some participants learn breath control by rotating from supported supine to prone positions or vertical to horizontal floating positions. With these individuals breath control may be learning "not to drink the water" as their mouths submerge.

Buoyancy and Floatation

A body in water is buoyed up by a force equal to the weight of the displaced water; a body floats when it displaces a weight of water greater than its own weight. The degree of floatation is dependent on the relative density of the body, lung capacity, and the ability to relax in the water. Fat or adipose tissue is less dense than muscle tissue so participants with lower percentages of body fat, persons with spastic or rigid cerebral palsy, experience floating difficulty. The greatest degree of floatation is achieved with the lungs inflated; sinking occurs as one exhales. The ability to relax and take regular full breaths enhances floatation capacity.

To float, a swimmer shifts from a vertical toward a horizontal position so that the body rotates around its center of buoyancy which is usually located in the chest area. This is achieved by moving the participant's center of mass, usually located in the hip area, toward the center of buoyancy. Raising the arms over the head (supine position) and/or flexing the knees toward the chest (prone position) accomplishes this adjustment. Buoyancy is usually taught with a prone and/or supine float as prerequisite(s) to propulsion skills. Persons who are "earthbound" or experience gravitational insecurity and hesitate to deviate from a vertical position (Down Syndrome), who can not adjust the relationship between their centers of buoyancy and mass (cerebral palsy or head injury), and who have limited sensation or limb control/loss (spina bifida or amputation) have difficulty achieving floatation.

A desired outcome is to maintain a horizontal or near horizontal body position. To do this a swimmer must be able to change positions and directions and recover, essential safety skills. Water games, aerobic exercises, and the practice of body shapes (tuck, pike, layout) encourage participants to experiment with buoyancy. Object recovery from the bottom or underwater determines the degree to which a swimmer is willing to overcome "earthboundness" and compensate for depth perception and spacial deficits. Swimmers are making a conscious effort to stay "grounded" when leaning rather than bending toward submerged objects, grasping the staff or stationary support (pool side), and/or extending the nonreaching hand out of the water as they reach for submerged objects. When the participant is required to move through a hula hoop or fall forward or backward, change in position is being practiced.

Personal floatation devices aid individuals who experience difficulty maintaining a floating position, such as those with cerebral palsy. The addition of these devices to one limb or one side of the body compensates for a tendency to roll to one side or float deeper on one side than the other as with the presence of amputations or strokes. Participants are also taught to compensate by turning their heads away from the affected side. When participants extend their arms and feet to maintain a prone or supine float, a degree of movement in the water sustains the float so gliding is introduced.

Floatation device assists individual with cerebral palsy to maintain a supine position.

Propulsion Leading to Basic Swim Strokes

Propulsion is the ability to move in the water. An arm stroke is the primary propulsive force with a kick-action contributing a supportive and stabilizing role. A plan of propulsion is based on the participant's physical capabilities. A swimmer is placed in a position that maximizes available propulsive forces (arm and leg movements). To illustrate, persons who are hemiplegic as a result of a stroke or head injury propel from a supine horizontal position by rotating to their unimpaired side and performing an underwater arm stroke and kick. With lower limb dysfunction, symmetrical strokes performed from a supine horizontal position like those used with the elementary backstroke maintain body alignment in the absence of effective kicks. With upper limb dysfunction, participants may elect to propel from a prone float position with rotation to a supine position for breathing.

When either arms and/or legs are unaffected, standard progressions are used to teach arm strokes and kicks. Finning and sculling the water with the hand and arm movements commence arm stroke instruction. Water pressure is felt on the palms of the hands and as the angle of the hand movement is varied, change in direction is also felt. An abbreviated "dog-paddle" stroke pulls the swimmer forward.

An effective kick gives support, balance, and a degree of propulsion. Participants are encouraged to kick from the hips. Hand-held devices like bar bell floats allow swimmers to concentrate on learning to kick. Participants who are hesitant to place their faces in the water learn to kick by back floating and holding these devices with extended arms in a supine position. With limited lower limb mobility, the use of swim fins increases ankle flexibility and helps strengthen thigh muscles used in kicking.

Usually the prone float and glide are followed by the back float and glide with kicking then finning and sculling added to maintain the glides. When some form of breath control is mastered through bobbing, the participant learns to exhale and/or hold the air, rotate/lift the head, and inhale above the water. A swimmer either turns the head from side to side, or lifts the head, or rolls from a supine to a prone position so adjustment to water hitting the ears and eyes occurs. While rhythmic breathing is practiced, either kicking or flotation devices and/or instructor support are used to stabilize and/or propel the body so symmetrical (elementary breaststroke) or alternating (crawl stroke) arm strokes are synchronized with head movement. As participants experiment with propulsion methods, safety turns, bobbing and endurance skills (distance swimming, maintaining a floating position) are practiced. Instruction is concluded with learning a survival float and to jump into deep water, level off, and propel to safety.

Above: Dog paddle is used as propulsion stroke.

Left: Distance swimming breathing is practiced using kickboards.

Aquatic Assessment

Directions: Prior to instruction, the participant/significant others are observed and/or interviewed to identify functioning abilities and factors having an effect on performance in the aquatic environment. Presence, date accomplished, or absence, left blank, of behaviors are reported and in some instances time/number of behaviors are recorded. Examples of how collected information is used follow the assessment.

Sensory Behaviors

Auditory

___Deaf

___Hard-of-hearing

___Hearing loss in ___R ear   in ___L ear

___Wears hearing aid

___Listens to speech

___Covers ears when hears loud noises

___Self-stimulates when hears loud noises

___Creates noise or echo in response to noises

Visual

___Blind

___Visually impaired

___Discriminates light and dark

___Discriminates shadows ___looks at light reflection on water

___Wears glasses in water

___Will wear ___won't wear goggles

___Will wear ___won't wear mask

___Opens and closes eyelids

___Looks at speaker

___Looks at objects in visual field

___Looks down ___does not look down into the water

___Watches objects move ___horizontally ___vertically

___Steps over ___does not step over lines or objects

___Reaches for support when looking down or stepping over

___Covers eyes to prevent water entry

Tactile

___Touches safety equipment ___touches floatation equipment

___Touches others ___resists touch of others

___Touches others only if controls the touch of others

___Holds objects

___Wears equipment

Speech and Breathing

___Creates audible speech ___number of words

___Cries ___Laughs

___Makes noise ___number of seconds

___Uses manual communication device ___computer to respond

___Drinks water   ___Licks water

___Allows water to move in and out of mouth for stimulation
___Breaths through mouth
___Breaths through nose
___Breaths through mouth and nose
___Breaths through mouth with nose pinched
___Closes mouth with nose pinched
___Opens mouth with nose pinched
___With nose pinched, holds breath, blows out for ___seconds
___With nose pinched, breathes in, blows out for ___seconds
___With nose pinched, blows out for ___seconds, breathes in
___Foams around mouth from swallowing air
___Enlarged tongue
___Able ___unable to open and close mouth
___NG Tube ___Tracheostomy ___Ventilator dependent
___False teeth ___Braces ___Plate ___Cleft palate

Self-Care

___Identifies personal belongings
___Dresses ___Undresses
___Toilets without ___with assistance
___Wears diaper
___Wears collection device
___Uses catheter
___Hair appears washed ___unwashed
___Places hands over face when hair is washed

Emotions Displayed

___Apprehension ___Fear ___Anger ___Aggression
___Happiness ___Confidence ___Trust ___Success

Social Interactions

___Holds hand(s) of others
___Talks with others
___Stays in ___withdraws from group
___Seeks to control group dynamics ___withdraws when not in controlling position

Cognitive

___Identifies directions: ___up ___down ___under ___over ___right ___left
___Identifies body parts
___Identifies safety and floatation devices
___Recognizes and responds to name
___Attends to task ___seconds
___Follows 1-2 step ___3-5 step directions
___Responds to verbal ___visual ___written directions
___Does not respond to verbal ___visual ___written directions
___Counts to: ___3 ___5 ___10
___Comprehends a count to: ___3 ___5 ___10

Motor

Stature

___Trunk long ___short

Muscle mass location

___Upper torso ___Lower torso ___Upper limbs (___R ___L)   ___Lower limbs (___R ___L)

Adipose tissue location

___Upper torso ___Lower torso ___Upper limbs (___R ___L)   ___Lower limbs (___R ___L)

Head Control

___Rotates head ___right ___left

___Lifts head from prone position ___from supine position

Balance

___Sits without ___with assistance

___Stands without ___with assistance

___Stands on ___R foot ___L foot

___Walks without ___with assistance

___Walks forward ___backward

___Runs forward ___backward ___zig zag

___Hops forward on ___R foot ___L foot

___Jumps forward ___backward with two feet off ground

Ambulation

___Independently

Ambulates with:

___Prothesis (___R ___L ___Both) ___Orthopedic device (___R ___L ___Both) ___Walker

___Crutches ___Wheelchair

Walks with:

___Even cadence ___On toes ___Heel to toe ___Feet inverted ___Feet everted ___Parallel arm swing

___Opposition arm swing

Hands/Arms/Shoulders

___Arms extended ___flexed

___Grasps ___Releases ___Claps

___Transfers objects from one hand to the other

___Crosses midline with R hand/arm ___L hand/arm

___Clamps down on top of instructors/others hand(s), arm(s)

___Shoulders broad ___narrow

Feet/Legs/Hips

___Legs extended ___flexed ___scissors position

___Legs long ___short

___Lifts R foot ___L foot off ground

___Squats at knees ___does not squat at knees

___Bends at waist ___does not bend at waist

Muscle tone

___Flaccid ___Spastic ___Contractures ___Uninhibited reflexes

Sleeping position
___Back ___Stomach ___Side ___Fetal

Dominance
___Right hand ___Left hand ___Right foot ___Left foot

Assessment Implications

Information is used to make adjustments in three areas:

1. Staffing. Example: When the self-care area lacks check marks, additional staff assistance occurs in the changing area before and after swimming.

2. Skill progression. Example: Steps in the breath control sequence are altered when the participant lacks head control. The selection of the nonambulatory or the ambulatory sequence is influenced by the participant's motor functioning.

3. Instructional techniques. Example: When hearing or visual impairments exist, safety procedures and teaching methods are altered.

**Acquisition of water safety skills
creates opportunities for
aquatic experiences such as sailing.**

SWIM PROGRESSION

Two sequences are presented. The first is used with persons who ambulate with or without the assistance of either an orthopedic or prosthetic device; the second is used with persons who ambulate with either an electric or nonelectric wheelchair or motorized device. Each sequence lists a series of tasks. The outcome is the ability to propel and remain safe in deep water areas. As the desirable outcome varies with each swimmer so does the use of each sequence. Thus, organization of the tasks might be altered to accommodate a swimmer's needs or the instructional intent. Results of the aquatic assessment guide instruction. Accomplishment of participant objectives is evaluated by progress along the skill sequences. Time to master each series of tasks is dependent upon each individual's experience.

Tasks are worded in terms of the skills performed by the swimmer. Unless otherwise noted, instruction commences in the shallow water. When appropriate, reference is made to usual strokes like the breaststroke or crawl. The term "with/without assistance" means that the instructor first aids the swimmer in task completion, then allows the swimmer to complete the task without assistance. The term "with/without support" means that the instructor first holds or stabilizes the swimmer as the task is completed then allows the swimmer to complete the task without support. Where reference is made to a floatation device, the equipment is a homemade or commercial item that is attached to or held by the swimmer.

Ambulatory

Adjustment to the Aquatic Environment

Walks into, through, and around the access and changing areas
Uses restrooms, changing stations, storage areas
Walks into and around aquatic area with/without assistance
Meets lifeguards and aquatic staff
Listens to safety rules and procedures
Sprinkles water on various body parts with/without assistance
Enters water with/without assistance
Stands and balances with feet on bottom with/without assistance
Walks around water perimeter with/without assistance
Walks through shallow water area identifying boundaries, entry-exit, depths with/without assistance
Walks into and through chest deep water with/without assistance
In chest deep water, maintains balance, sculls hands underwater
In chest deep water, runs, jumps, hops various directions
Instructor swishes or rotates swimmer from R to L, front to back, with water covering shoulders downward
Places water on back of head, then R and L ears, then top of head, then eyes with/without assistance
Puts goggles on with assistance
With/without goggles on, retrieves objects above/on/under water with/without assistance
Exits water with/without assistance

Breath Control

(Completes tasks in chest deep water with or without goggles and with eyes open)

Upon command, inhales above water, submerges entire head (bobs) vertically, with mouth open or closed and with or without blowing bubbles, does not ingest water, resubmerges with assistance

First step is to orient swimmer to aquatic setting.

Movement exploration facilitates water adjustment.

Swimmer adjusts to water on head.

Swishing helps swimmer overcome defensiveness to water on various body parts.

Practices bobbing until individualized consistent breathing pattern in vertical position is established with assistance

In waist deep water grasps objects floating in the water with one hand, then both hands, keeping hands under water with/without assistance

In chest deep water repeats above

Upon command, submerges vertically, grasps/touches under water objects, maintains breathing pattern, with assistance

Buoyancy and Floatation

(Completes tasks in chest deep water with or without goggles and with eyes open)

Upon command, submerges vertically, sits on bottom, holds breath or blows bubbles, resubmerges to breathe with/without assistance

Upon command, submerges vertically, grasps/touches objects on bottom with one hand, then both hands, keeping both hands under water, maintains breathing pattern, with/without assistance

Upon command with instructor's support, takes breath, tilts forward as feet slide backwards, moves downward and forward, upper torso touches the bottom (sky dives), resubmerges to vertical position

Sky dives independently

Standing vertical position, forms arm circle, tucks one knee then second into circle, lowers head forward into water, sustains position until body stabilizes in tuck float, recovers to vertical position with/without assistance

Bobbing sequence, top to bottom and below: Instructor demonstrates as swimmer observes breathing pattern, swimmer and instructor then complete bob together.

Tuck float sequence: Swimmer overcomes earthboundness as floatation skills are acquired.

Standing vertical position, extends arms/hands forward underwater, submerges face forward above eye level, breathes, looks forward with/without assistance

Pushes into prone float position, sustains a minimum of one body length, recovers to standing position with/without assistance

Pushes into prone float position, sustains position with arms extended, feet together, holds breath or blows, recovers independently

Propulsion

(Completes tasks in chest deep water, moves to deep water,
with or without goggles and with eyes open)

Pushes into prone glide position, holds breath or blows, kicks (flutter, whip, frog or dolphin), recovers to vertical position with/without assistance

Pushes into prone glide position, holds breath or blows, kicks, dog paddles (human stroke) with underwater arm recovery, recovers to vertical position with/without assistance

Repeats above attempting symmetrical arm movements like breaststroke

Repeats above attempting alternating (crawl) arm movements

Practices rhythmic breathing with selected prone position arm and leg strokes with/without assistance

With support in shoulder level water, clasps hands behind small of back, tilts backward, water covering ears, arches back, raises hips, walks then lifts feet as moves into back float position, recovers to vertical position

From above position, extends arms shoulder level with palms toward bottom, assumes back float position, recovers to vertical position with/without assistance

Glides into back float position, kicks (flutter, whip, frog or dolphin), recovers to vertical position with/without assistance

Glides into back float position, kicks, fins, continues glide, recovers to vertical position with/without assistance

Repeats above attempting symmetrical arm stroke like elementary backstroke

Repeats above attempting alternating arm stroke (back crawl)

Practices selected back glide stroke (legs only, arms only or combination of both) with recovery with/without assistance

In shallow water, swims in prone position to R then to L takes one breath with/without assistance

At water level arm's length above head, breathes, submerges vertically, touches bottom, resubmerges with/without assistance

Repeats at various depths in deep water sustaining breath control

In deep water, swims in prone position to R then to L, takes one breath, with/without assistance

In deep water, from back glide position, takes one breath, completes vertical turn to prone position, swims to safety with/without assistance

In deep water, from prone glide position, takes one breath, completing vertical turn to supine position, swims to safety with/without assistance

In deep water, from prone glide position, takes one breath, completing horizontal roll to back glide position, swims to safety with/without assistance

In deep water, from back glide position, takes one breath, completes horizontal roll to prone glide position, swims to safety with/without assistance

Completes deep water bob, surfaces, takes one breath, swims in prone position to safety with/without assistance

Jumps into deep water, takes one breath, levels off, swims R or L to safety with/without assistance

Practices distance swimming with/without assistance

In deep water, maintains survival float position, lifts head to breathe with/without assistance

In deep water, maintains back float or inverted "C" position with explosive breathing with/without assistance

Swimmer pushes into prone glide position, as instructors demonstrate and observe.

Swimmer practices breathing with flutter kick.

Swimmer practices alternating arm stroke.

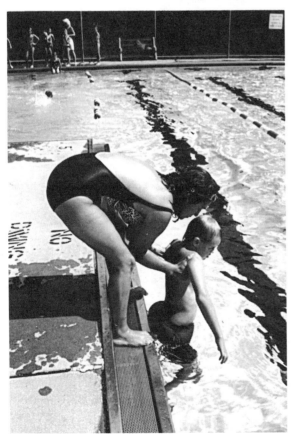

Swimmer is prepared to move to deep water swimming by being dropped into water of increasing depth.

Nonambulatory

Adjustment to the Aquatic Environment

Moves into, through, and around the access and changing areas
Uses restrooms, changing stations, storage areas
Moves into and around aquatic area with/without assistance
Meets lifeguards and aquatic staff
Listens to safety rules and procedures
Enters water with assistance
Moves around water perimeter with assistance
Moves through shallow water identifying boundaries, depths, accessibility features with assistance
Moves into chest deep water with instructor support
Instructor swishes or rotates swimmer from R to L, front to back, with water covering shoulders downward
Places water on back of head, then R and L ears, then top of head, then eyes with/without assistance
Puts goggles on with assistance
Moves through water with/without goggles and assistance retrieving objects above/on/under water
In chest deep water, grasps/touches underwater objects with/without goggles with assistance
Exits water with assistance

Water entry sequence with individual with physical impairment.

Nonambulatory swimmer is moved into chest deep water for instruction.

Above and right: Instructor swishes swimmer to encourage adjustment to water.

Breath Control

(Completes tasks in water chest deep with or without goggles and with eyes open)

Upon command, nose pinched, breathes into instructor's palm, repeats to establish breathing pattern

Upon command, nose pinched, submerges entire head (bobs), does not ingest water, resubmerges with assistance

Repeats bobs until breathing pattern is consistent with/without nose pinched with assistance

In prone horizontal position with support, moves through water, resurfaces to inhale

Repeats with intermittent instructor support for increasing lengths

With support, assumes supine position

Sustains stable back float position with/without arm and leg movements with assistance

Rotates head to preferred side from back float position with assistance

Rotates 360 degrees from supine to supine, breathing, with assistance

Rotates 180 degrees from supine to prone position, breathing, with assistance

Rotates 180 degrees from prone to supine position, breathing, with assistance

Supine position with support is a prerequisite to breathing, floating, and propulsion with individual with physical impairment.

Stable back float position is assisted by instructor.

Buoyancy and Floatation

(Completes tasks in water chest deep with or without goggles and with eyes open)

In prone horizontal position, moves from one instructor to another, establishes floatation position with momentum provided by instructors
Repeats with roll from prone to supine position without recovery with assistance
Repeats roll with recovery, maintains stable water position, with/without assistance
Repeats with roll from supine to prone position without recovery with assistance
Repeats roll with recovery, maintains stable water position, with/without assistance
Sustains back float position with recovery to stable position independently
Sustains prone float position with recovery to stable position independently

Top to bottom: Swimmer porpoises between instructors to experience buoyancy and floatation.

Propulsion

(Completes tasks in chest deep water, moves to deep water,
with or without goggles, and with eyes open)

Assumes back float position, kicks (flutter, whip, frog, dolphin, or scissors) with assistance

Assumes back float position, kicks, fins or sculls, with assistance

Repeats above attempting symmetrical arm stroke like elementary or European backstroke with assistance

Repeats above attempting alternating (back crawl) arm movements

In supine position, practices selected arm and leg strokes with/without assistance

Assumes prone float position, water above eye level, holds breath or blows, kicks (flutter, whip, frog, dolphin or scissors) with assistance

Pushes into prone glide position, holds breath or blows, kicks, dog paddles (human stroke) with underwater arm recovery, recovers to vertical position with/without assistance

Assumes prone float position, holds breath or blows, kicks, attempts symmetrical arm stroke like breaststroke with assistance

Repeats above attempting alternating (crawl) arm movements

In prone position, practices selected arm and leg strokes with/without assistance

In deep water with/without assistance practices bobbing with individual breathing pattern

In deep water practices selected back strokes with/without assistance

In deep water on back changes direction from R to L with/without assistance

In deep water rotates 360 degrees from supine to supine, breathing, with/without assistance

In deep water, breathes, completes horizontal roll from supine to prone position, swims to safety with/without assistance

In deep water completes horizontal roll from prone to supine position, breathes, swims to safety with/without assistance

In deep water from back glide position completes vertical turn to prone position, breathing, swims to safety with/without assistance

In deep water from prone glide position completes vertical turn to supine position, breathing, swims to safety with/without assistance

In deep water, from prone glide position changes direction from R to L with/without assistance

In deep water, maintains survival float position with/without assistance

In deep water, maintains back float or inverted "C" position with explosive breathing with/without assistance

Practices distance swimming with/without assistance

In deep water, takes one breath, levels off, swims R or L to safety, with/without assistance

Propulsion in prone glide position is enhanced with floatation support.

INSTRUCTIONAL TECHNIQUES

Teaching suggestions found successful with ambulatory and nonambulatory swimmers are presented. Suggestions related to equipment use and bobbing are applicable to both ambulatory and nonambulatory swimmers. Each list is sequenced from entry through propulsion skills. The concluding list presents strategies used with particular needs. Further suggestions are offered by type of disability in the next section of the manual.

Teaching Strategies—Ambulatory

Complete the aquatic assessment prior to and during initial contacts with swimmer/significant others; observations out of the water are helpful in predicting responses in the water

As swimmer enters and exits, assess functioning, observe degree of confidence and fear expressed in motor and verbal behaviors

Entry is affected by refraction when the swimmer sees the bottom; swimmer might be more hesitant to enter pool than lake; instructor from underwater touches swimmer body parts to orient swimmer to effects of refraction

Hula hoops and working with partners help swimmers adjust to the size of the water area as they help control spacial relationships; hoops also help the group stay together

Hearing loss is compounded by water entry, may be exhibited as behavior problem; instructor relies on demonstration and maintains eye contact with swimmer

To determine a swimmer's buoyancy, in shallow water, have the swimmer hold the breath in a prone position for a count of 5 to 10; repeat with an exhale; observe the body parts that submerge, they are nonbuoyant; to compensate the instructor encourages the swimmer to become more proficient with the nonbuoyant limbs and to overcompensate with the already stronger limbs

Buoyancy is experienced with initial water contact; encourage swimmer to stand in chest deep water so effects of buoyancy on balance are felt; swimmer's hands are held underwater (instructor's hands on top) so water pressure pushes up

Water depth at chest level is desirable as this is the level at which the water gives the most support to the swimmer; if this depth is not available to the participant, the instructor swishes the swimmer from right to left and front to back to identify if the swimmer is defensive on a particular side and to experience the effects of buoyancy

Instructor positions self in front of and facing swimmer to create a vacuum through which swimmer moves more easily

Dislike for having water on head/eyes might be reflective of eye surgery, trauma, visual impairments, or extensive medical intervention to that area; others object to having water on their faces as they have had few previous experiences, someone else has washed their hair or they have covered their faces; adjustment occurs slowly and without being splashed in the face

Partners help each other adjust to the water.

If participant exhibits difficulty walking, running, jumping, hopping, the swimmer practices the correct way to perform each of these tasks as this helps stroke coordination

Goggles are used to enhance adjustment; persons who exhibit tactile defensiveness resist their use

Steps for goggle use: swimmer feels goggles, looks through goggles, places on eyes without strap, places strap on back of head with goggles sitting on forehead, slides goggles down over eyes, looks through; defogs when cloudy, washes in baby shampoo to keep lens clear

Prone strokes practiced with swimmer looking at target.

Breath holding and/or pressure on the face is contraindicated with persons having respiratory, visual, head trauma, or cardiac issues, so use of mask or goggles might be inappropriate and rhythmic breathing is adjusted to develop exhalation rather than breath holding

Swimmers are encouraged to keep eyes open as balance, coordination, safety, movement in the water are enhanced, instructor wears goggles to see swimmer; if swimmer's head is down rather than looking forward and if head is rotating and arms are slapping water, the eyes are probably closed

The ultimate goal of bobbing is to have the swimmer take a breath above water then exhale under water through the mouth and nose; from the assessment tool, the instructor ascertains the speech and language pattern which reveals whether a rhythmic pattern is likely; the goal of bobbing can be accomplished without a traditional rhythmic breathing pattern, i.e., the swimmer may keep the mouth open yet never ingest water

Bobbing is taught upon command so instructor's lead helps swimmer establish a breathing pattern

Bobbing is taught several ways depending upon the functioning ability of the swimmer; with swimmers who have severe cognitive and motor impairments, the process is begun with water being poured over their heads, the instructor counts 1, 2, 3, then makes a noise as the water is poured; underwater this swimmer is taught to make a noise as the instructor counts so blowing is learned

Instructor helps swimmer develop breath control during bobbing.

Bobbing with swimmers standing in chest deep water; instructor demonstrates with one of swimmer's hands on instructor's head, the second hand in front of the instructor's face, instructor counts 1, 2, 3, continues to blow on swimmer's hand as submerges and resurfaces; instructor then places hands on swimmer's shoulders with swimmer placing hands on instructor's shoulders, upon command both submerge and resurface

Floatation devices are not used to teach buoyancy and floatation skills as a swimmer's buoyancy is altered; these devices are used during propulsion to enhance movement by stroke correction or helping the swimmer maintain a prone or supine horizontal position to better complete individualized strokes

Swimmer who pulls instructor through the water feels the effects of viscosity and water density on floatation

To experience floatation, the swimmer holds the prone float position for a count of 10 then exhales

Floating positions are more easily sustained with slight kicking/finning

Buoyancy is increased by inhaling during recovery phase of a stroke with continuous exhalation during stroke completion, this also keeps water out of the swimmer's nose

Nonbuoyant swimmers, persons with cerebral palsy or large quantities of muscle mass, prefer the inverted "C" position or back float rather than prone float

Recovery from a supine position to standing position is taught by having swimmer pretend to pull a chair up then sit down upon the chair

Practice of prone float and strokes with swimmer looking at a forward target helps swimmer maintain correct head position in the water

Objective with arm stroke instruction is to determine whether symmetrical or alternating is best, depends on ability to coordinate strokes and use both sides of body; breathing and leg movements are then added to the stroke

To help coordination, the instructor adds momentum by pushing swimmer forward in outstretched position

Swimmer standing on deck with a kickboard stretched overhead to the count of 10 helps instructor judge body alignment and swimmer concentration which then are evident as strokes are practiced in the water

To determine the swimmer's preferred side for breathing, stand in front of swimmer and have swimmer turn head; observe side to which head is turned most frequently—this is preferred side

Splashing during strokes is sign of improper swimmer movements, for example, with the flutter kick heels only break water on prone strokes, toes only break the water on back strokes

Swimmer learns to recover to vertical position from supine position.

Practice stroking in a gliding rather than a stationary position; kicking while holding wall might be confusing as swimmer does not feel effects of swimming at the water surface on stroke development

When swimmer lacks ankle flexibility, develop a whip or frog rather than a flutter kick

When flutter kick is a kick from the knee rather than kick from the hip, swimmer is turned to the side to practice the kick as the water density self-corrects the knee kick

Instruction in deep water helps swimmer concentrate and focus on instructor and model other swimmers, and the addition of new skills from the sequence is easier than in the shallow water

To help adjustment to deep water, the instructor encourages the swimmer to keep eyes open and hands under water to compensate for the feet not touching the bottom

Survival float is individualized as it depends upon each individual's buoyancy; tucking the knees to chest in the prone position makes swimmer more buoyant; placing the arms overhead in the water in the back position (inverted "C") also adds buoyancy

Practice distance swimming with definitive beginning and ending points so swimmer concentrates on proper breathing and stroking and feels secure moving between concrete points

When swimmer experiences difficulty with propulsion, recheck skills from the first three phases of the progression, especially eyes open, bobbing with consistent breathing pattern, and independent floatation position

Equipment used for prone and back or supine strokes (arms are always extended with equipment use):

Bar bell—grasp is easier than pinch used to hold kickboard, it provides stability and is used with lifting head to breathe and learning to flutter kick

Kickboard—rotate head to breathe, instructor has swimmer drop shoulder and roll head so ear turns onto instructor's hand

Bottles—used with person with broad shoulders, one arm extended forward and second at side, in prone position rolls to breathe

Fins—used to correct flutter kick, recovery is difficult because fin lengthens the leg; once kick is corrected, remove as swimmer tends not to move the arms; fins allow swimmer to lift head to breathe

Floats—attached to the swimmer's back allow continuous swimming in prone position

Hula hoops—as swimmer changes direction from R to L swims through hoops yet if swimmer has perceptual deficits, the hoop tends to clutter the environment and add to the impairment

Various devices can be used to help develop skills; here kickboards are used to develop leg strokes.

Teaching Strategies—Nonambulatory

Entry-exit into the aquatic area consumes swimmer energy and may affect the amount of time the swimmer remains in the water as the aquatic experience also requires additional energy expenditure. Swimmers with less adipose tissue will more easily chill and, therefore, may not remain in the water for extended time periods; adding light-weight long sleeve shirts and pants retains body heat.

When the swimmer is transferred into the water, persons completing the transfer release the swimmer when water covers the swimmer's shoulders as this minimizes the effect of gravity. The instructor in the water is in at least chest deep water to support the use of the instructor's back during swimmer entry. When the swimmer enters/exits via a ladder the lead down the ladder is with the affected leg and up the ladder with the nonaffected leg. Following are some useful teaching strategies for nonambulatory participants.

Placement of a mat at entry-exit points allows swimmers to sit as they slide into the water, experience water adjustment with water being sprinkled over their heads, and/or dry-off before returning to a wheelchair after water exit

Prosthetic and orthopedic devices are protected from exposure to the sun and water by covering them and removing them from water's edge; this also protects the user as the devices become hot to touch and cause blisters if "wet rubs against dry" when replaced on the swimmer

Swimmer's wheelchair prepared for re-entry after swimming.

Wheelchair is protected from sun during aquatic experiences.

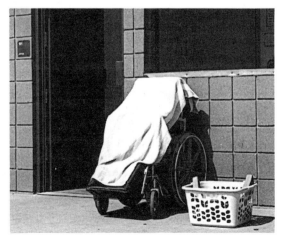

Water entry sequence: Staff encourage independent entry with mat to protect swimmer.

Swimmers supported in a vertical position at chest deep water level experience the effects of buoyancy; water walking (movement in a vertical position) is possible even if swimmer does not walk on land because the water is 800 times more dense than the air

Most swimming is taught with the instructor in front of and facing the participant as the drag created enables easier swimmer movements; if swimmer is aggressive or unable to control arm movements, the instructor may choose to remain behind the swimmer; when supporting the swimmer, the instructor keeps the elbows tight against the sides of the body

Swishing or rotating the swimmer right to left and front to back determines if the swimmer resists or is defensive in a particular position, often the back; instruction commences on the nondefensive side or position with continuous effort to develop strokes on the nonpreferred side; swishing also develops the trunk muscles

The nose is pinched with swimmers who experience difficulty with speech or breathing or closing their mouths; these swimmers might also use a Laxto nose clip or mask until a breathing pattern is established or indefinitely while swimming

Bobbing with swimmer who can not stand and/or experiences gravitational insecurity is taught by holding the swimmer under the arm pits, counting 1, 2, 3, submerging, blowing on swimmer's chest, resubmerging; then swimmer and instructor repeat together; gravitational insecurity tends to be more prevalent with persons who self-ambulate than those who rely on ambulation assistance

Steps for mask use: place mask on instructor to demonstrate that breathing can not occur through the nose, place mask over swimmer's face unattached, place pressure on mask and feel the swimmer's breathing pattern, when pattern is regular place strap over the swimmer's head, breathe above water in stationary position then move and breathe and observe swimmer's breathing pattern; when hair is under mask, mask will not seal; vaseline on moustache allows mask to seal

Bobbing is a safety skill to be acquired by swimmers even if the swimmer only uses supine strokes and/or back float in the water as the skill, if needed, allows the swimmer to resubmerge to a back float position and propel to safety

Breath control is acquired by moving the swimmer in a "porpoise" manner between two instructors, the swimmer is "lifted" to breathe, the degree of support is reduced and the distance between instructors is increased as the swimmer's breath control improves; swimmer also determines whether the head is lifted or rotated or a horizontal roll (when head can neither be lifted nor rotated) is used for breathing; the instructor initiates this breathing practice with count of 1, 2, 3, so a consistent pattern is established and maintained

Recovery during floatation requires the use of the nonaffected limbs to maintain balance while initiating direction change and supplying the momentum to avoid injury to affected limbs; instructor teaches swimmer to scull to facilitate this recovery

If participant experiences difficulty with supine recovery, instructor teaches swimmer to roll to prone side then complete the recovery

Body rolls in the direction of the head turn, the instructor teaches the swimmer to roll to preferred side, keeping the legs and arms close to the body with one leg crossed over the top of the other in the direction of the turn

Prone strokes, swimmer breathes to the affected side so the nonaffected side (limbs) propels the swimmer

Propulsion commences with back rather than prone strokes as breath control is not an issue; yet an ultimate goal is to enable an effective stroke with individualized rhythmic breathing

Propulsion is enhanced with the use of fins, especially if one side is dominant (persons with strokes); if the foot position in the fin is rigid or flexed the fin is probably uncomfortable and actually inhibits movement; after placing fins on a swimmer, allow the swimmer to wear the fins for a few moments then check for redness (improper fit)

Floatation belts are used to stabilize swimmers if they tend to roll to one side or the other; this permits effective use of the arms and/or legs

Long distance swimming is made possible with the use of snorkels when swimmers experience difficulty breathing (can't lift or rotate their heads or roll horizontally)

Inverted "C" is the preferred survival stroke with persons with physical impairments; swimmers practice slowly so they maintain their desired water position

Swimmer porpoises under water to gain breath control.

Teaching Strategies—Specific Individuals

Gravitational Insecurity or Earthboundness

Evident with Down Syndrome individuals and persons with severe multiple impairments who have experienced limited movement

Swimmers experience difficulty entering the water, climbing up and down the ladder; the instructor guides the swimmer's feet

Water adjustment begins with the swimmer's feet on the bottom; movement away from this base of support is resisted

Adjustment to the water by sitting on the side is discouraged as this confuses the swimmer and does not address the issue

Adjustment time is increased, swimmer walks, jumps, picks up increasing numbers of sticks at various water depths, jumps into hoops, practices keeping both hands under the water and bending forward as sticks are retrieved

Sequence to acquire floatation skills:

        pick up one stick from bottom in waist deep water

        complete above with instructor holding outstretched hand or placing the outstretched hand under the water

        pick up two sticks from bottom with two hands

        pick up a group of sticks with both hands

        pick up five or more sticks arranged in a straight line on the bottom (swimmer moves forward, bending as sticks are grasped)

        sit on the bottom of the pool then sit with hands on the bottom

        from prone position, hold instructor's hands, release, then regrip

        complete above with stationary object, e.g., pool wall

        complete sky dive

        prone float with instructor's support then without to stationary object

Swimmer is allowed to return to the side or wall after completing instructor directed tasks until confidence permits movement through the water without return to the reference point

With the swimmer in the water, pouring water over the head or squeezing a sponge over the head are techniques used to feel water on the face

Persons may prefer to swim under the water than at the surface because the effects of their insecurity are not felt so time to acquire prone and back glide strokes is increased

Prone strokes are preferred as the back position is one in which the swimmer becomes defensive

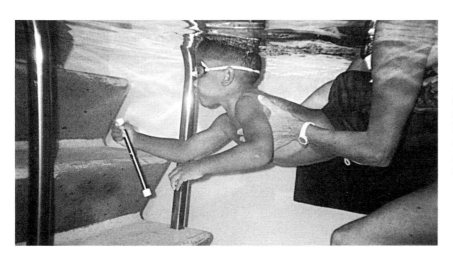

For an individual with gravitational insecurity or earthboundness, buoyancy and floatation skills are acquired by retrieving objects under water.

Cognitive Impairments—Autism

Shallow water progression is ineffective as swimmer does not learn by imitation

Swimmer may hesitate to enter water so instructor helps swimmer enter

Swimmer has a natural eggbeater kick with a vertical swim position, head is not submerged as swimmer expresses tactile defensiveness; swimmer may also cough after face is submerged and resist the use of goggles, therefore, bobbing is taught after the swimmer develops prone propulsion

Deep water swimming permits the use of fins which reinforce natural kick;

Child with autism is closely monitored by staff.

swirling or flapping motion of hands (self-stimulation) is redirected to dog paddle, floats are attached to back, swimmer develops prone propulsion in this manner; swimming toward target in deep water also controls attention

Swimmers dislike noise which contributes to self-stimulation so classes are small or instruction is one-on-one; when the swimmer presses both ear lobes inward with the thumbs this might indicate the area is too noisy

Persons with Hemiplegia, Paraplegia, Quadriplegia, and Circulatory Impairments

Water pressure on the chest wall negatively affects breathing and causes fear

Prior to water activity, physician identification of resting heart rate and recommended pulse rate range is desired

Instructor monitors fatigue level by observing tremors, pulse rate, change of color in face and extremities

Breath is taken to affected side with arm and leg strokes completed by unaffected limbs

Breath holding is avoided by rolling from prone to back to breathe

If fins are used, swimmer walks backwards; recovery to standing position is difficult with fins as they lengthen the legs

Recovery to standing position might also be difficult due to increased buoyancy caused by adipose tissue

If swimmer uses an alternating arm stroke like a crawl, the swimmer's legs either "fishtail" or move in an "S" pattern, either of which impairs forward movement; thus symmetrical strokes like the breaststroke are recommended

SWIM LESSON PLAN

After review of each participant's swim forms and completed assessments, the instructor uses lesson plan forms to plan each session's content and instructional processes.

Instructor (name):_____

Participant(s)(names):_____

Program name and date:_____

Session objectives(s):_____

Introductions/Warm-up/Safety check:
    Welcome participants
    State daily objectives and review aquatic rules
    Observe physical, psychosocial behaviors
    Identify warm-up exercises:_____

Review Previous Experience
    Identify participants' skill levels
    Practice skills from previous class:_____

Demonstrate New Skills:
    Present next skill(s) on progression
    Individualize skill demonstration
    Individualize teaching methods
    List new skills and teaching methods:_____

Practice New Skills
    Organize participants
    List practice drills/exercises:_____

Tapering Off
    Identify individual experience/exercise:_____
    Identify group experience/exercise:_____

Debriefing
    Individual swimmer skill demonstrations
    Instructor summarizes accomplishments
    Instructor observes swimmers' physical, psychosocial behaviors
    Participant dismissal and assist with clean-up

Staff Evaluations
    Recording of participant progress
    Recommendations for revision of objectives, content, teaching strategies: _____

Follow-up
    Report to supervisor
    Actions regarding swimmers:_____

BEHAVIOR MANAGEMENT
IN THE AQUATIC ENVIRONMENT

In the aquatic environment, the instructor, like a classroom teacher, establishes instructional parameters prior to actual "teaching." Controlled participant behavior is expected to avoid injury or damage to participants, staff, and equipment and to maintain program quality. Behavior management techniques are used to set expectations and support controlled participant behaviors. Behavior management encourages positive behavior by providing positive reinforcement for appropriate behavior and negative reinforcement for inappropriate behavior.

Examples of positive applications of behavior management include:

1. Minimize rules and express them positively: Rather than state what you don't want done, state what is expected. Say "Listen when the instructor gives directions" rather than "don't enter the pool before the instructor tells you what to do."

2. Eliminate negatively worded statements. Change "if you don't listen to the instructor you will sit out" to "when you listen to the instructor you can enter the pool."

3. Help the participant to make the connection between appropriate behavior and positive consequences. Say "because you listened to the instructor you entered the pool quicker."

4. Instill a sense of accomplishment and recognition of success in order to encourage participation; show excitement over success. Motivate continued improvement with "high fives," handshakes, and "show me that breath control one more time."

Principles of positive reinforcement include:

1. The reward should be immediate so it is clearly associated with the appropriate behavior.

2. Frequent reinforcement is more effective, initially, followed by less frequent reinforcement.

3. The reward is given for achieving a skill rather than complying with the instructor's demand.

4. Rewarding approximations of the desired skill is one way to encourage skill development.

5. Instructors may use a desired activity like diving as a reward following a less enjoyable activity like stroke practice.

Structuring the Environment

The environment and factors external to the participants and instructor influence the use of behavior management techniques. Therefore the instructor structures several features of the aquatic environment:

1. "Down time" between activities is filled with transition games, songs, stunts, demonstrations. Organization for the next activity has either occurred while participants were active in the previous activity or prior to instruction. Undesirable behavior occurs when participants are expected to "wait patiently."

2. Equipment is placed out of sight or reach and distributed to participants after directions/demonstrations are complete.

3. The leader maintains "proximity control" by remaining in the water, preferably, or near the participants to observe signs of frustration, fatigue, fear, aggression, and self-defeating behaviors. The next activity is initiated when one or more of the participants display or contribute to off-task behaviors.

4. A schedule, routine, and consistency create secure feelings and alleviate fear. Change produces uncertainty and behavior problems. To compensate when change is inevitable, plan with participants, prepare them prior to the deviation, and show them, for example, the consequences of rain and cool air on the water temperature.

5. Set and consistently enforce reasonable limits of acceptable behavior realizing that fun happens; for example, splashing is fun yet harmful when someone's recovery to a safe vertical or horizontal position is affected.

Techniques for Handling Behavior

Harmful or dangerous behaviors do occur and leaders must apply negative reinforcement. Agencies vary in their tolerance of inappropriate behaviors. Generally, physical contact (corporal punishment), confinement in an enclosed area, and/or physical restraint are prohibited. When a person is dismissed or removed from the aquatic environment, if applicable, the proper caregiver and/or authorities are informed. Appropriate risk management forms are also completed and filed with a supervisor.

A total lack of response, or planned ignoral, is effective in managing some disruptive behaviors. Consistent ignoring or nonrecognition generally decreases a behavior; this assumes the behavior is harmful to neither the participant nor others. For example, hitting a kickboard when the desired instructor's attention is not forthcoming may cease when the leader ignores the action.

Another technique used with mildly disruptive behaviors is a sign or motion like a downward hand motion with the palm down signifying silence or an "excuse me" with immediate participant eye contact. This action minimizes disruption and attention to the negative behavior and allows the participant to gain control and realize the leader is in charge. Immediately following with a motion or word to encourage participant attention to the task reinforces desired behaviors.

Undesirable behavior is stopped when the actions could lead to injury to participants, staff, or others, damage equipment or the facilities, and/or prevent continuation of the activity. One approach is to use a "time-out" from the activity to allow the person to regain control—it is not used to restrict participation. Points to remember as disciplinary action is contemplated include:

1. Consequences of undesirable behaviors are enforceable. For example, threats like "no meal or snack" are unrealistic when the swim leader is not responsible for this function.

2. Disciplinary action is focused on the behavior rather than the participant. For example, "Your unwillingness to follow directions is inappropriate and can cause you harm. Listen so you will be safe. We want you to learn to swim."

3. Consistency is critical. Similar behaviors have similar consequences with all participants and equal treatment is given to all involved.

4. Leaders avoid emotional responses to negative behaviors. They might state, "This is upsetting to me; your splashing hurts other swimmers who are not as skilled as you."

5. Negative behaviors escalate during confrontational situations . In "win-lose" situations, remove the participant from the group so dignity is retained and others are not upset.

Behaviors Requiring Management Strategies

Types of behaviors requiring management are presented below, with possible management solutions:

Acting Out Behaviors

Bullies others, fights, hits, bites, throws equipment, refuses to obey the leader, abuses self, shows off, displays temper tantrum.

Solutions: Redirect or divert the act toward harmless activity like flutter kicking or race to the other end; ignore; let participant know you understand the reason for the behavior, which may or may not be associated with the aquatic activity; reward acceptable behavior, allow participant to select (lead or demonstrate) swim activity.

Nonparticipatory Behaviors

Anxious, tense, refuses to participate, daydreams, says "I can't do it," withdraws, lacks enthusiasm.

Solutions: Allow additional water adjustment time; present alternative activities with participant choice; perform games or exercises that release energy; set aside place to which participant may withdraw; use assessment information to determine swimmer skills and initiate activity from that point; identify successes to foster participant feelings of security.

Resistive Behaviors

Withdraws, strikes out, denies, rejects, sets unrealistic goals, criticizes others, loudly announces nonparticipation, won't try new skill, sits and refuses to move, spits, kicks, runs away.

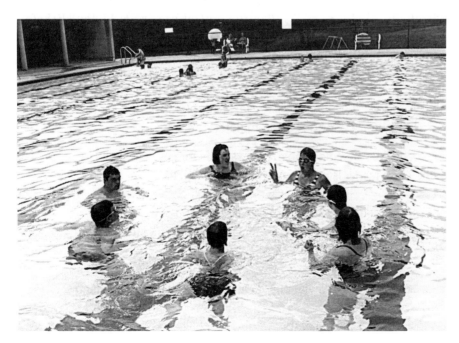

Instructor uses circle formation to organize class in shallow water.

Solutions: Let participant know an attempt is OK and does not have to be perfect; praise acceptable behavior; set limits, that is, it's OK to strike the water or kickboard but spitting results in leaving the water; present choices, such as stay with class or complete the activity after other swimmers; do frequent buddy checks and head-counts.

Excessively Active Behaviors

Hyperactivity, restlessness, wanders, jumps or bounces, spins self or objects, throws toys and teaching aids, pushes others, unable to complete a coordinated stroke pattern.

Solutions: Provide personal space and quiet spots, alternate activities (bobbing with swimming distances); move activities between water and deck or beach; alternate group and individual activities; encourage show and tell and allow participants to be leaders.

Attention Seeking Behaviors

Demands leader's attention, splashes, strikes out, talks loud, throws equipment, wants to be first, shows off.

Solutions: Set limits; use firm verbal commands with choices; reinforce good performance; be shock-proof to foul language; assign tasks; incorporate show and tell time and encourage group recognition of participant successes.

Instructor uses line formation to organize class in deep water.

Swim Program Considerations for Individuals with Disabilities

This section contains information on individuals with disabilities. To organize the immense amount of material while not compromising the integrity of each individual, a system similar to that found in the study materials of the National Council for Therapeutic Recreation Certification, Inc. is used. Within each of the six diagnostic groups (cognitive, physical, sensory, emotional, social, and addictions), information on each impairment is organized as follows: population descriptors, swim program precautions, and practical applications.

The authors acknowledge that the descriptions are neither all inclusive nor comprehensive. The attempt is to present information about the more prevalent disabilities and to cite programmatic needs unique to the aquatic environment.

Although swimming is usually recommended for persons with disabilities, medical prescription and infection control policies warrant special supervision, caution, and individualized planning. Swimming can be contraindicated in the following situations: Active or chronic infections, such as STDs, sinusitis, osteomyelitis, rheumatoid arthritis, ear problems, allergies, open wounds or sores like bed sores, and circulatory problems. With persons who wear treatment devices like ostomy collection devices or prostheses, or use assistive devices like inhalers for asthma, staff assess the aquatic setting and swimmer and make accommodations to enable participation.

Cognitive Impairments

Autism

Population Descriptors

Autism is a severe form of pervasive developmental disorders with onset in infancy or childhood usually noticeable before age three. It is characterized by impairments in social interactions, verbal and nonverbal communication, and activities and interests. Displayed behaviors may include: Self-stimulation, repetitive movements, hyperactivity, avoidance of human interaction and touch, single word communication, lack of startle response and eye contact, out-of-sequence actions, inappropriate use and/or fixation on objects, aimless movements, and unawareness of environmental safety issues. Autistic-like behaviors are found with persons with other cognitive and emotional impairments.

Swim Program Precautions

1. The aquatic environment may cause sensory overload/underload resulting in behaviors like "acting-out," resistive behaviors, withdrawal into "their own world." Noise level, light reflection, waves, and water movement contribute to such behaviors.

2. Unawareness of safety issues, inability to attend, and aimless wandering necessitate supervision in and around the setting.

3. The tendency to avoid touch affects the use of floatation devices for instruction and safety.

4. Training to discriminate auditory and visual safety cues is fostered with repetition and consistency during instruction.

Practical Applications

1. Structured movement and vigorous exercise reduce self-stimulatory behaviors.

2. To gain attention, establish eye contact, allow swimmer to return to referent point after successful task completion. Floatation devices in the deep water promote positions conducive to attending and skill development using the swimmer's natural abilities.

3. Nonverbal communication and physical prompting are most effective.

4. Facilitate reduction of stimulatory behaviors with initial water adjustment periods prior to attempting instruction.

5. Use of colored water toys holds attention and aids instruction.

6. Use exhibited behaviors like turning or spinning as starting points for brief intermittent instruction.

7. Techniques recommended with other cognitive impairments are also effective with youth with autism.

Learning Disabilities

Population Descriptors

A person with a specific developmental disorder or learning disability experiences inadequate development in specific academic, language, speech, and motor skills. There is a noticeable discrepancy between potential ability and actual performance. A learning disability is a secondary impairment with physical impairments like cerebral palsy and social impairments like abuse. Observed behaviors include distractibility, hypo-hyper-activity, impulsivity, low-frustration tolerance, uncoordinated movements, dissociation, visual and auditory memory deficits, and perceptual-motor deficits.

Swim Program Precautions

1. Establish routine, structure, and compliance with safety rules prior to water entry. Once in the water, follow a routine, organize each activity, and minimize transition time between activities as participants become distracted without structure.

2. Control the number of participants and objects in the actual instruction area.

3. Focus on general form rather than precision, as frustration builds and diminishes attention when coordination is emphasized.

4. Establish boundaries with concrete objects like lane markers or hula hoops, so perceived space is reduced.

5. Emphasize start-stop signals to compensate for perseveration and distractibility and to ensure safety.

Practical Applications

1. Have swimmers demonstrate so instructor is available to encourage others to focus on modeled behavior.

2. A circle formation provides structure and opportunity for modeling others.

3. Perceptual motor deficits affect depth and distance perception. Use markers to facilitate participant awareness of varying pool depths and distance between self and the "end."

4. Demonstration of the whole skill followed by practice of each step encourages participants to see relationships. Synchronize verbal directions with demonstration; for example, show the right arm as "pull with this side" is said, yet minimize the use of words.

5. Set up concrete individualized rewards to correspond with steps on the progression. Include recognition in each session.

6. Include in the initial warm-up skills from previous sessions as skill acquisition varies from session to session.

Mental Retardation

Population Descriptors

Mental retardation is defined by degrees of deficit in intellectual functioning and adaptive behavior that are evident during the developmental years (prior to age 18) and continue throughout one's life. The degree of deficit is noted by defined levels:

Mild mental retardation is generally noticed by school age and affects the largest percentage of those with mental retardation. Basic academic skills are acquired yet independence is affected by social skill acquisition and job maintenance.

Moderate mental retardation is noticed prior to school age and is associated with distinguishing features like Down Syndrome. Motor and social skills are affected and academic skills remain fundamental. Supported living and vocational choices prevail.

Severe and profound mental retardation is represented by the smallest percentage of those considered mentally retarded. Secondary and multiple impairments are evident. Assistance with language, self-care, movement, and expression of emotions is needed.

Swim Program Precautions

1. Some form of communication and compliance with safety rules and procedures are prerequisites to skill instruction.

2. Medical concerns like seizures, heart conditions, atlantoaxial subluxation, ear tubes, and medication side effects affect participation.

3. Bowel and bladder accidents are controlled by toileting prior to entry and by wearing protective diapers that tolerate warm water (do not decompose).

4. Participants with severe and profound retardation lack a self-preservation instinct or comprehension of dangers inherent in the aquatic environment so assistive devices and one-on-one supervision are employed.

5. Instruction is made concrete as abstract concepts like buoyancy are not comprehended. Skill repetition and training rather than reasoning facilitate performance. The swimmer does not necessarily associate the ability to float with the amount of muscle mass and adipose tissue.

Child with mental retardation models instructor's actions.

6. Restate and practice compliance with aquatic rules when the setting changes as swimmers may not transfer information.

7. Newness and/or change in the aquatic environment can precipitate self-abusive or aggressive behaviors that result from fear or loss of security felt in a familiar setting.

Practical Applications

1. Physical guidance combined with verbal cues aid swimmers in comprehending how to perform skills.

2. The use of task analyzed sequences are self-reinforcing; thus, following the steps in the progression facilitates skill development.

3. Unwillingness to deviate from a vertical position or earthboundness (gravitational insecurity) is one focus of water adjustment instruction; as a consequence, additional time is devoted to the initial progression steps.

4. Emphasizing "eyes open under water" compensates for perceptual motor impairments.

5. Movement exploration (jumping, walking, turning) allows participants to experience cause and effect relationships between body parts and their movements.

6. Objects like floating and nonfloating sticks and hoops encourage participants to develop an awareness of directions and space and their body positions. This awareness is needed prior to developing strokes that propel swimmers through the water.

7. As participants are uneasy with change, time allowance to become familiar with the environment in and around the aquatic area is planned into each session. A participant statement like "no" or "I don't want to" might really mean, "this new situation is uncomfortable to me."

8. Social skills and communication are developed through water games and sports. Fitness is enhanced with endurance and aerobic activities. Both types of experiences are appropriate to include in each session.

9. Response to emergency drills is practiced during sessions and compliance with safety procedures is consistently expected.

10. Progress along the sequence may level off and/or regress. Repetition using different strategies, such as games or assistive devices, fosters skill maintenance and progression.

Severe Multiple Impairments

Population Descriptors

Persons with more than one lifelong cognitive, physical, sensory, emotional, and social impairment that are interactive and have cumulative effects are described by this term. Representative individuals include: dual diagnoses like mental retardation and mental illness, cerebral palsy-deaf, deaf-blind, and mental illness with alcoholism. Behavior characteristics include: mobility impairments, abnormal reflex retention, ineffective communication and reality awareness, self-care limitations, limited range of motion and use of the senses, tense/rigid appearance, unresponsiveness, and a tendency to become overstimulated.

Swim Program Precautions

1. Rigid muscles are relaxed when water temperatures range from 86 to 90 degrees and air and humidity are controlled.

2. One-on-one supervision (buddy system) facilitates movement through water and through a full range of motion.

3. Instruction emphasizes safety and the ability to establish and control a body position in the water to ensure breathing.

4. The aquatic environment either calms and/or encourages increased activity level. As a consequence, structure, routine, consistency, and compliance are used to reinforce desired behaviors.

5. Planning considers factors like seizures, medication side effects, presence of personal assistive devices, participant fitness level, and the events that precede and follow the aquatic experience.

Practical Applications
1. The aquatic environment provides "movement freedom" and an atmosphere conducive to relaxation. However, splashing and the effects of light reflection and refraction can adversely stimulate the swimmer.

2. Spacial awareness is acquired when the instructor uses positional words like up, down, over, and under to describe movements and actions in relation to body position in the water.

3. Passive range of motion exercises build strength while aerobic activities like walking and kicking increase fitness.

4. Walking-falling-recovering in the water facilitate ambulation and avoidance of injury out of the water.

5. Water sports like volleyball and basketball encourage social skill development and physical well-being not as accessible out of the water.

6. Stroke form is de-emphasized while movement and self-control are the foci of instruction.

7. Progress may come slowly so feedback and individualized concrete rewards are part of each experience.

Physical Impairments

Musculoskeletal—Amputations

Population Descriptors
A congenital amputation is absence of a limb or part of a limb at birth while an acquired amputation is loss or removal of a limb or part of a limb after birth. When the joint remains intact, use of artificial limbs (prostheses) are more likely. Balance is affected by limb loss. Functioning ability is influenced by number of missing limbs, level of amputation, and portion of the limb remaining. Bilateral amputations later in life have a greater impact as adults must redefine their self-images while youth have little with which to compare their losses. The visual appearance of residual limbs could affect responses of other aquatic participants.

Swim Program Precautions
1. Assistance with removing/replacing artificial limbs is given with care as each is unique, expensive, and fitted to the wearer.

2. Either improper fitting or placing a dry prosthesis against a damp limb results in rubbing which causes decubitus ulcers (bed sores).

3. Additional assistance is given during water entry when participants leave artificial limbs in the changing area.

Practical Applications
1. To overcome balance deficits, participants use devices like hand-held floats or kickboards.
2. Propulsion is maximized with the use of fins and hand paddles.
3. During water adjustment, participants adapt to perceptual impairments by doing underwater activities, negotiating obstacles, and moving in varying water depths.

4. With upper limb involvement, scissors and whip kicks are used in propulsion with a sidestroke or finning action.

5. With lower limb involvement, the glide portion of strokes is emphasized using backstroke or breaststroke. A flutter or whipping movement of the torso aids in direction and propulsion.

6. Breathing occurs as the swimmer turns opposite the intact or strong side and/or as the swimmer thrusts forward and lifts the head.

7. Without lower limbs, swimmers tend to be buoyant and have difficulty diving below the water surface. Buoyancy is also noticed when the swimmer enters the water; the residual portion of the limb is often buoyant and floats to the surface.

Musculoskeletal—Arthritis

Population Descriptors

Arthritis means inflammation of the joint. Swelling, stiffness, redness, and pain within the joints, muscles, and connective tissues result. Rheumatic forms of arthritis are chronic and have no cure. Unpredictable periods of intensity and remission with fatigue characterize arthritis. Several forms of arthritis are prevalent: Rheumatoid arthritis affects adults and youth; usually affects many joints and is characterized by inflammation. Osteoarthritis or degenerative joint disease (natural aging outcome) affects local joints, usually weight bearing, yet is rarely characterized by inflammation. Systemic arthritis affects the entire body. Peripheral arthritis affects only joints, most commonly the knee.

Swim Program Precautions

1. Movements that increase joint pain, such as fast-paced kicking, are contraindicated. Participants are taught to discriminate between muscle stiffness and joint pain.

2. Water entry and exit is an area of concern due to wet surfaces, unsteady gaits, or fear of falling. Chair lifts, handrails, and personal assistance relieve anxiety and trauma potential.

3. Increased water and/or air temperatures and water resistance contribute to fatigue. Intermittent rest periods are planned.

Water exercise remediates impairment attributed to arthritis.

4. Since the joints might be traumatized during a dive, caution is recommended.

5. Weather conditions/changes affect joints and range of motion. Participant responsiveness might be reflective of environmental factors.

Practical Applications

1. Standing, walking, and moving various body parts against water resistance may be the primary program objective rather than swim skill development.

2. Warm water exercises performed with a slow steady rhythm relieve stiffness, reduce pain and joint swelling, and increase range of motion and strength.

3. Range of motion exercises not only prevent loss of motion but decrease joint deformity.

4. Propulsion through the water occurs with adapted strokes when the range of motion of affected limbs is limited; for example, sidestroke and scissors kick are used.

Musculoskeletal—Muscular Dystrophy

Population Descriptors

This related group of diseases progressively weaken voluntary muscle groups and result in a bulky appearance caused by replacement of muscle fiber by connective tissue. Onset is usually during youth. As the disease progresses, mobility, self-care, and fitness are reduced and participants become susceptible to respiratory infections. The more prevalent forms include: Duchenne or pseudohypertrophic, a false appearance due to enlarged tissues in the upper and lower limbs; facio-scapular-humeral, most common adult form with weak facial muscles followed by weakness in shoulder and upper torso then lower extremities; and limb-girdle, frequent lower limb involvement with the shoulder girdle affected.

Swim Program Precautions

1. Increased susceptibility to respiratory infections requires precautions to avoid chilling, including moderating water and air temperatures, drying quickly after water exit and immediately putting on warm clothing, and avoiding extremes between water and air temperatures.

2. Caution in transfers is necessary as participants, in later stages, lack control and strength in the shoulder and thigh muscles to assist with the transfer.

3. Due to weakness in the girdle areas, excessive pulling of the limbs during transfers can cause dislocation of the shoulder and hip.

4. With weakness in the neck and shoulders, the participant experiences difficulty raising the face to clear the water to gain air during breathing.

Practical Applications

1. Swimming maintains strength in unaffected muscle groups which prolongs independence. Flexion contractures are also decreased and respiratory endurance is increased. Independent movement occurs longer in swimming.

2. Range of motion exercises and movement exploration counter joint deformities.

3. Skills to emphasize early in the instructional program are balancing, walking (floating), and recovering to either the feet or a supine position to acquire air.

4. The elementary backstroke with finning and sculling and dolphin and/or flutter kick from a supine position remain effective throughout the course of the degeneration.

5. Floats add stability and enable use of remaining limb function.

6. Passive range of motion exercises counter contractures.

7. Fatigue exacerbates progression of the impairment so intermittent rest periods are incorporated.

Musculoskeletal—Spina Bifida

Population Descriptors

Spina bifida is a defect in the spinal column caused when one or more of the vertebral arches fails to close around the spinal cord. Location and extent of the lesion determine the degree of impairment. The degree to which the spinal cord protrudes through the opening determines the form of spina bifida.

In spina bifida occulta and spina bifida meningocele motor and sensory impairments are not necessarily apparent while in spina bifida myelomeningocele motor dysfunction is evident. Paralysis and loss of sensation in the lower extremities result. Secondary consequences include incontinence, spinal column deformities, obesity, skin lesions (bed sores), urinary tract and renal infections, and hydrocephalus when excessive amounts of fluid accumulate within the cranial cavity.

Swim Program Precautions

1. Participants may use wheelchairs and leg braces for mobility and wear devices for bowel and bladder collection. Transfers are completed with utmost care to avoid either damaging the devices or the participant.

2. When braces are removed, participants might need back support and protection of the lower limbs as a cut or scrape is slow healing and susceptible to infection. Participants wear socks to avoid injury to their feet. Due to a lack of sensation, swimmers are unaware of scrapes or cuts, for example.

3. If external collection bags are present, some are removed with the catheter clamped off while in the water.

4. When a shunt is present (tube surgically implanted behind the ear to drain cranial fluid into the chest cavity), care is taken to avoid a direct blow to either the back of the head or chest area.

5. If there is an imbalance between upper and lower body weight, participants have a difficult time righting themselves from supine positions in the water; as a consequence fear of activities completed on their backs might prevail.

6. The bones of the lower extremities fracture easily so care is taken to protect against injury/damage.

Practical Applications

1. Focus of instruction is on strengthening muscles to improve posture and increasing lung capacity. Improved circulation also helps prevent/heal bed sores and aids in elimination of body wastes. With improved upper body strength, independent transfers and self-care are enhanced.

2. During initial instruction periods, participants practice losing and regaining upright, prone, and supine positions to ensure breath control and water safety.

3. Strokes in the supine position with underwater recovery are most effective. Back float and elementary backstroke with sculling and finning are used in propulsion. Bilateral strokes are more effective.

4. Floatation devices are used to offset balance problems.

Nervous System—Cerebral Palsy

Population Descriptors

Cerebral palsy (CP) originates prior to or during birth and/or in infancy as a result of brain damage. Weakness, paralysis, poor muscle tone, and a lack of coordination are primary characteristics. Reflexes are either uninhibited or exaggerated resulting in the appearance of limited muscle control. Secondary impairments include cognitive, sensory, language, and seizure disorders. Symptoms describe the various forms of cerebral palsy:

Spasticity, most prevalent: Hypertension, muscle contractures, scissors gait, jerky movements, and postural deviations.

Athetosis, second most prevalent: Uncontrollable constant involuntary movement, affecting primarily head and upper limbs, movements intensify with excitement and subside with relaxation.

Ataxia: Balance deficits, uncoordinated movements, staggered walking, poor muscle tone.

Rigidity: Stiffness, hyperextension of body parts, muscle tightness resists efforts to move the affected limb(s).

Tremor: Involuntary, uncontrolled, rhythmic pendular appearing movements.

Mixed: Presence of more than one form of cerebral palsy, identified as a severe multiple impairment.

Swim Program Precautions

1. Warm water is desirable (86-90 degrees) as the amount of muscle activity is reduced resulting in more normal postural tone and increased relaxation (necessary prior to stroke instruction). Transfer between changing and water areas is affected by varying air temperatures which cause muscle activity and tension.

2. Fear of falling is exaggerated in the aquatic environment with slippery floors, depth perception deficits, and decreased buoyancy. Supervision during transfers and while in the water is important.

3. Noises and movements that trigger either a startle response or reflex actions create muscle tension and can cause the head to submerge. A calm environment and instructor support of the participant's head and shoulders help to maintain relaxed muscles and breath control.

4. Movements that increase tension like the flutter kick or head extension are contraindicated. As a consequence, floating is difficult.

5. Floatation devices are used as movement aids rather than life saving devices; use considers the degree to which range of motion is restricted. Supervision is important as an unexpected noise or wave could cause the head to submerge.

6. With reduced lung capacity, expiration of ingested water is difficult. As a consequence, precautions to avoid "drinking" the water are important.

Practical Applications

1. Swim skill development is influenced by degree of movement ability, degree of breath control, and degree of relaxation.

2. Establishing a communication system between the instructor and participant is a first order of business as impaired speech affects understanding of participant's oral expression.

3. Although movement potential is greatest in the horizontal position, during water adjustment an upright body position is attempted. This aids depth and buoyancy awareness and practice of falling and regaining a balanced position.

4. In chest deep water, assisted walking and bobbing are accomplished. These exercises enhance mobility and respiratory endurance.

5. Water orientation in a supine position follows vertical positioning. With the instructor at the participant's head supporting the head, neck, and shoulders, body alignment is maintained, eye contact enhances secure feelings, and a draft is created by the instructor's body. From this position, breathing, propulsion, and stroke recovery are easier.

6. Effective horizontal movements include finning, sculling, breaststroke, and elementary backstroke. Slow symmetrical movements are easier (whip kick).

7. If the knees draw toward the chest, slow muscle massaging and passive range of motion aid extension. Slower strokes foster relaxation which results in more propulsion. Telling the participant to relax can cause tension. Demonstrate muscle tension by having the swimmer feel the instructor's arm as the instructor makes a fist.

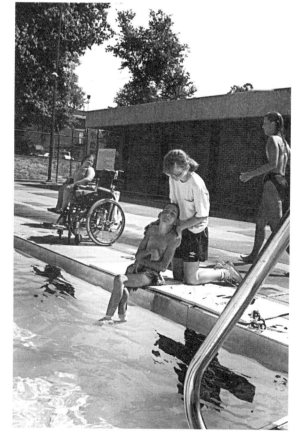

Swimming alleviates spasticity evident in cerebral palsy.

8. Length of time in the water is influenced by overall warmth of the environment; wind, humidity, and air and water temperatures affect muscle relaxation. Wearing clothing in the water maintains body warmth.

9. A goal of participation is independence, so if adding a floatation device increases balance, buoyancy, propulsion, and/or water time, use is justified.

10. To help gain lip closure for breath control, the head is slightly flexed and in a position other than a supine position as this promotes the mouth opening. Humming helps lip closure. Blowing bubbles occurs after lip closure.

Nervous System—Cerebral Vascular Accident (Stroke)

Population Descriptors

Interruption to the flow of blood through the brain causes a stroke. Hemiplegia and hemiparesis are the overt signs of a stroke. Right side brain damage causes left hemiplegia or paresis (weakness); left side brain damage causes right hemiplegia or paresis.

A person who is a left hemiplegic experiences difficulty interpreting visual information, orienting to the surrounding environment, and performing perceptual motor skills.

A person who is a right hemiplegic experiences difficulty understanding spoken and written language and retaining, recalling, and recognizing information, and is sensitive to the disability.

Both right and left brain damage cause visual neglect, contractures, spasticity, seizures, and shoulder subluxation.

Swim Program Precautions

1. If participation occurs through a cardiac rehabilitation program close monitoring/documentation of heart rate, blood pressure, and energy expenditure is likely.

2. Establishing the degree of comprehension and judgment is critical as participants are unaware of their deficits or instructor requests/directives and tend to either over- or under-estimate their capabilities.

3. Although desirable, warm water activity contributes to fatigue, evident with tremors and heightened seizure activity.

4. Comprehension deficits affect, for example, understanding how to hold one's breath or how to protect oneself when in deep water; perceptual deficits affect awareness of body position in the water, water depth, and distance between self and water's edge.

5. Visual neglect limits the participant's ability to see on the affected side, so proximity to that side is unknown as is instructor demonstration that occurs on that side.

6. Fear of falling and experiencing breathing difficulty are heightened when surfaces are slippery and as the water reaches chest deep level; both require assistance.

7. A first step is to determine whether dominance of one side or the other exists as behaviors and personalities vary; persons with nondominant paralysis usually respond more adequately to instruction than do those with either right or left dominance.

Practical Applications

1. Aquatic activity in warm water reduces spasticity (which can be painful), increases strength and stamina, improves range of motion and endurance, and encourages freedom of movement. Bilateral movements and spacial awareness (e.g., movement through hoops) counter neglect and incoordination.

2. During water adjustment, nonverbal communication cues are established so meanings are properly interpreted. Initiating activity in chest deep water aids balance and breath control.

3. An adapted crawl or free style stroke using the uninvolved limb for propulsion with the uninvolved body side in the water is effective. Breathing to the affected side is usual.

4. Mood fluctuations, embarrassment from incontinence, and depression affect the participant's responsiveness.

5. Range of motion exercises maintain normal joint movement and counter shoulder subluxation and stiffness. Passive range of motion of the affected limb by the instructor helps reduce muscle contractures.

6. Continual practice of returning to either a vertical or supine (horizontal) position in the water helps participants feel comfortable in the water.

7. Water walking improves balance, stamina, and endurance.

8. Rhythmic breathing helps speech and increases the expiration component of breathing.

9. Use of fins facilitates propulsion.

10. Flexion activities, body tuck, and flutter kick can enhance contractures; rapid movements also contribute to muscle tension and spasticity. Slow deliberate actions and full range of motion around the joints are therefore encouraged.

11. Wearing a nylon sock protects the involved foot.

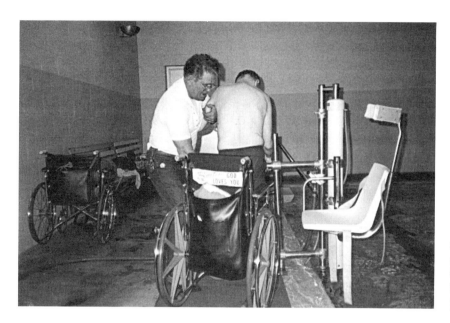

Chair lift allows swimmer with stroke to enter water safely. See also illustrations on pages 59 and 76.

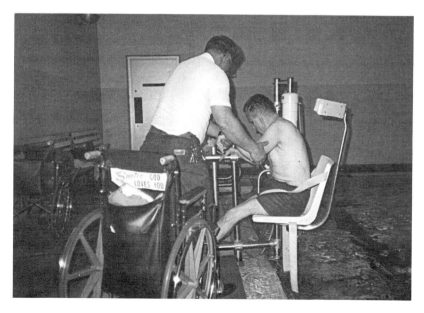

Nervous System—Seizure, Convulsive Disorder, Epilepsy

Population Descriptors

A seizure is a sudden change in consciousness or behavior characterized by involuntary motor activity. A seizure may be a one-time occurrence (as that which happens with alcohol withdrawal) and may accompany other disorders like cerebral palsy, brain injury, and severe mental retardation. Epilepsy is a diagnostic category describing a group of syndromes with repeated seizures. Thus not all persons with seizures have epilepsy. Seizures are described by the amount of involvement.

Partial seizures begin in one specific body part and travel to others with (complex partial) or without (simple partial—Jacksonian or psychomotor) loss of consciousness, jerky muscle contractures, or short-term behavioral changes resulting. Generalized seizures involve several or all body parts. Absence or petit mal is characterized by brief loss of consciousness while tonic-clonic or grand mal is evidenced by rapid jerky movements, loss of consciousness, and sleep or a coma stage.

An aura or reported warning sign such as an unusual odor precedes some seizures. Medications like tegretol, dilantin, and depakene impede motor functioning yet control seizure activity.

Swim Program Precautions

1. Lifeguard on duty should be made aware of persons with active or uncontrolled seizures (medication controls much seizure activity).

2. Springboard diving is contraindicated as a seizure while on the board could result in a dangerous fall. Supervision monitors activity that could result in head trauma.

3. If a seizure occurs in the water, the primary need is to keep the participant's face above water so breathing occurs. Loss of bowel/bladder control might require temporary clearance of other participants from the water and addition of chemicals.

4. If water is taken in as the seizure occurs, expulsion of air/digestive tract contents causes choking so staff hold the participant's head to prevent swallowing of vomitus.

5. Placement of mats/blankets near the water's edge provides comfort and warmth during recovery.

Practical Applications

1. Conditions in the aquatic environment can trigger seizures: extreme temperature changes, excitement, intense reflections off the water, and hyperventilation.

2. An akinetic or drop seizure happens quickly and staff must learn to distinguish it from routine bobbing and prone floats. Observation of participant's underwater activity is important. A swimmer who has had a drop seizure while in the water may be moving in the water after the seizure due to the water activity of other swimmers.

3. Seizures use energy so the time allowed to swim is adjusted to avoid fatigue.

4. A lack of coordination and varied energy levels result from seizure medication; supervision monitors abrupt changes or unexplained behaviors which could warn of seizure activity.

Nervous System—Multiple Sclerosis

Population Descriptors

Progressive degeneration of the nerve fiber coverings (myelin sheaths) and replacement with scar tissue throughout the body impairs the ability of the brain to transmit messages. Periods of intensification and remission occur so diagnosis is difficult. Other symptoms include: Impaired vision, speech and swallowing difficulties, fatigue, partial to complete paralysis, and loss of bladder/bowel control and coordination. As the disease progresses, seizures, spasticity, and tremors in the lower limbs occur.

Swim Program Precautions
1. Warm water is not easily tolerated (above 86 degrees).
2. Participants tire more easily after exertion.
3. During remission, depression affects motivation levels.
4. Length of the illness and stage of intensification or remission affect cognitive and motor functioning.

Practical Applications
1. Water walking enhances endurance and reduces muscle stiffness.
2. Relaxation, stretching, and breathing exercises reduce muscle tension, a factor in spasticity and tremors.
3. Circulation is improved with aerobic activity; this reduces the likelihood of bed sores.
4. During initial swimming periods, practice of recovery from prone and supine positions to an upright stance and prone to supine positions facilitates breath control. Orientation to the setting is planned if visual impairments exist (auditory warning signs are established).
5. With the presence of paralysis, floating, finning, and sculling are encouraged.
6. Stroke recovery above the water is used with impaired throat and neck muscles.
7. Demonstration accompanies verbal information to ensure comprehension. A request to the participant to repeat or model instructor actions affirms a swimmer's awareness level.
8. If the swimmer is not able to recover from a supine to vertical position, the swimmer rolls to a prone position then recovers.

Neuromuscular—Spinal Cord Injuries (SCI)

Population Descriptors
Spinal cord injuries result in motor and sensory impairment below the level of the lesion. The extent of the impairment is determined by the level at which damage occurs and the severity of the damage to the cord. An incomplete lesion from bruising, crushed, or torn nerve tissue causes partial or incomplete paralysis. Complete paralysis and loss of function results from complete spinal cord severance. Also lost is sympathetic nervous system control that affects heart rate, blood pressure, and body temperature controls. Spasticity, which is painful, is more evident with incomplete than complete paralysis. Level of injury and number of limbs involved define spinal cord injuries:

Paraplegia involves the legs and is caused by damage at or below T2 (second thoracic vertebra); the lower the level of the lesion the greater the upper body strength and function.

Quadriplegia involves four limbs and is caused by damage above T2; movement is absent or limited in all four limbs and breathing is difficult.

If injury occurs at several levels, more functioning on one side of the body than the other is possible. Extended rehabilitation periods create complications: Pressure sores, urinary and bowel irregularities, contractures, spasticity, osteoporosis, edema, and respiratory and cardiovascular impairments.

Swim Program Precautions
1. Swimming provides possible risk of injury to limbs lacking sensation so protective nylon socks/clothing are worn to prevent scrapes slow to heal.
2. Internal and external collecting bladder/bowel devices are clamped-off/emptied prior to water entry.
3. Proper horizontal water positioning allows breathing and prevents inhalation of water.
4. With high level injuries, little neck and head control is present so staff stand behind the participant's head, grasping the shoulders and bracing the head between their lower arms.

5. A participant's response to staff and the aquatic experience is affected by emotional state; depression, anger, fear, and low self-esteem result in lowered enthusiasm and motivation.

Practical Application
1. Warm water promotes relaxation and helps to offset spasticity.
2. Walking, stretching, and pushing against resistance counter contractures and develop upper torso strength.
3. Bilateral strokes from a supine position and European and elementary backstrokes, with underwater arm recovery, are best.
4. Balance and buoyancy problems and drag created by nonfunctioning limbs are managed by using arm and leg floaties. Degree of leg movement is enhanced with swim fins.

Neuromuscular—Traumatic Head (Brain) Injuries (TBI)

Population Descriptors
TBI is an insult to the brain caused by an external force that produces either diminished or an altered state of consciousness (coma) and either temporary or permanent impairments in cognitive, physical, sensory, and behavioral functioning. Impairments are similar to a stroke, that is, damage to the right side of the head causes left side impairments and vice versa:

Left cerebral hemisphere injury or right hemiplegia affects language and comprehension; response to a new situation is slow, disorganized, and anxious.

Right cerebral hemisphere injury or left hemiplegia affects judgment and visuo-perceptual functioning; persons tend to be self-centered, overestimate their abilities, deny their impairments, and are insensitive to the needs of others.

Additional issues include: Spasticity, contractures, fatigue, balance and sensory disturbances, impulsivity, incontinence, emotional lability, apathy, depression, and personality changes.

Rehabilitation programs address the recovery levels defined by the Rancho Los Amigo cognitive functioning scale:

Level 1 — No response
Level 2 — Generalized response
Level 3 — Localized response
Level 4 — Confused, agitated
Level 5 — Confused, inappropriate, nonagitated
Level 6 — Confused, appropriate
Level 7 — Automatic, appropriate
Level 8 — Purposeful and appropriate

Swim Program Precautions
1. As the level of cognitive functioning improves, less structure, fewer demands (more choices), and less one-on-one supervision are needed.
2. Warm water helps relaxation and reduces spasticity yet contributes to fatigue so time in the water is closely monitored.
3. Stimulation from noise, waves, and people is distracting so instruction is best in controlled settings.
4. Perceptual deficits affect balance, depth perception, and awareness of self in relation to objects and others; staff supervision and visual markers direct participant movements.

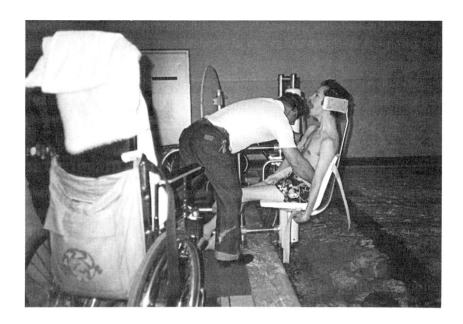

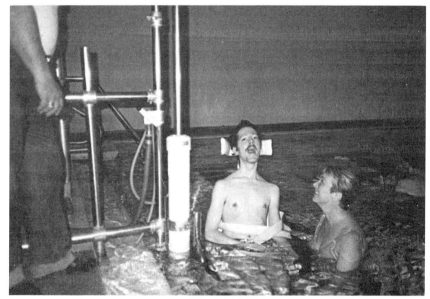

**Aquatic experiences improve muscle tone and strength with individual having head injuries.
A lift is used to transfer swimmer to water safely. See also illustrations on pages 55 and 76.**

Practical Applications

1. Aquatic experiences improve coordination and breathing, strengthen muscle groups, encourage relaxation and release of frustrations, and aid circulation which helps reduce bed sores.

2. Reality orientation, repetition, modeling, physical and verbal cues, behavior management, and frequent redirection of behaviors and reinforcement are teaching strategies.

3. Water adjustment includes relearning balance and the effects of gravity and self-testing so realistic goals are set.

4. Supine positions with bilateral movements and floaties are used during propulsion.

Circulatory System

Population Descriptors

Cardiovascular diseases affect the heart and/or blood vessels and are either primary impairments or result from other diseases like diabetes. The heart controls blood circulation which in turn provides nourishment for the entire body; thus, impairment in the heart impacts total well-being. Several forms of heart and blood disorders are organized for convenience:

Congenital heart diseases are either present at birth or result from illnesses like rheumatic fever and are caused by either malformation in the heart structure or large blood vessels near the heart. Following surgery a child experiences little or no limitations; prior to surgery disease is characterized by breathing difficulties, chest pain, fainting, edema, and cyanosis around the mouth.

Acquired heart disorders occur after birth. Disorders include coronary heart disease or atherosclerosis, hypertension (high blood pressure), and arteriosclerosis. A heart attack or myocardial infarction (MI), when the blood supply to the heart is cut off, results from these disorders. Angina pectoris (chest discomfort), shortness of breath, edema, dizziness, fatigue, and depression characterize these disorders.

Hemophilia is an inherited disease characterized by repeated bleeding. Bleeding into the joints, especially knee, ankle, and elbow, results from bruises or other trauma. A clotting factor is injected to manage bleeding. Splints used to prevent joint bleeding cause limb contractures and limit range of motion.

Anemia results from reduced oxygen-carrying capacity of the blood. Persons at risk are those who experience difficulty with food intake, cerebral palsy, or severe mental retardation. Fatigue, irritability, and lowered activity levels are noticed.

Swim Program Precautions

1. Pulse rate and blood pressure are monitored during cardiac rehabilitation.

2. To control dampness, humidity-temperature index, and wind chill, programs are either indoors or atmospheric conditions are considered.

3. Injury potential is monitored as is bluish coloration around the mouth ((skin discoloration might indicate an injury is causing uncontrolled bleeding; or if the swimmer is cold, the lips turn blue).

4. Length of sessions is monitored to avoid fatigue.

Practical Application

1. With graduated exercises energy expenditure is monitored.

2. Bobbing and water adjustment emphasize breath control to build cardiovascular muscles.

3. Initial propulsion occurs in shallow water areas with upper torso out of the water (supine rather than prone position) and emphasis on leg rather than arm strokes.

4. Water walking and jogging increase aerobic capacity.

5. Flexion and stretching exercises encourage relaxation.

Close monitoring is required for swimmers with any heart disorder.

Respiratory System

Population Descriptors

Impairments in the nose, lungs, pharynx, larynx, trachea, and bronchi cause breathing difficulties. A medical connotation of chronic obstructive pulmonary disease (COPD) is used to identify chronic bronchitis, emphysema, asthma, and cystic fibrosis:

Chronic bronchitis is an inflammation of bronchi of the lungs characterized by frequent coughing and expulsion of sputum.

In emphysema, walls of the alveoli lose elasticity and tear leaving large inefficient air spaces; regardless of number of breaths taken, oxygen in the bloodstream is lacking. One consequence is heart failure.

Asthma or bronchial asthma is characterized by swelling of the mucous membrane lining bronchial tubes, excessive secretion of mucus, and spasms of the bronchial tubes. A hacking cough, wheezing, and dyspnea exist. During an asthma attack, obstruction might become severe and require medical attention.

Cystic fibrosis (CF) is an inherited childhood disease. A thick sticky mucus secreted by the internal organs clogs the bronchial tubes and lodges in the windpipe obstructing breathing and impeding digestion. A salty sweat is produced by the sweat glands.

Swim Program Precautions

1. Lack of adipose tissue causes CF child to chill quickly.
2. If outside, pollens, smoke, or dust can trigger attacks.
3. With salty perspiration, sodium chloride supplements are used.
4. Pre-exercise medications and warm-up routines facilitate proper breathing during water activity.

Practical Applications

1. During water adjustment and breath control sessions, diaphragmatic breathing exercises improve expiration capacity.

2. Arm strokes are emphasized to develop shoulder and abdominal muscles. Swim mitts and paddles increase resistance and are beneficial in muscle strength development.

3. With CF, a barrel chest and kyphosis develop; swimming actually inhibits this action. Helpful strokes are the inverted breaststroke, elementary backstroke, and back crawl.

4. Physical activity causes expiration of sputum, so staff encourage children to cough up dislodged fluids.

5. Water jogging and walking improve endurance.

Endocrine and Metabolic Disorders

Population Descriptors

Over or under activity of the pituitary, thyroid, and adrenal glands (endocrine glands) causes obesity and growth deviations.

Diabetes mellitus, a chronic metabolic disorder, affects all body systems including circulatory and nervous with secondary complications like kidney and heart disease, amputations, and blindness. Type I or Brittle Diabetes, juvenile onset or insulin dependent, is caused by not enough insulin and higher than normal sugar levels which cause weight loss. With Type II, maturity or adult onset or noninsulin dependent, the body is unable to use insulin, causing high blood sugar levels.

Insulin shock, reaction, or hypoglycemia is due to low blood sugar levels and too much insulin, which can be caused by exercise. Characteristics include sweating, nausea, headache, raised pulse rate, rapid onset; requires sugar, Life Saver, Coke.

Diabetic coma or ketoacidosis is marked by slow onset and lack of insulin, and is more critical than insulin shock. It is characterized by fatigue, thirst, leg cramps, abdominal pain, and eventually unconsciousness.

Swim Program Precautions
1. Snack consumption (carbohydrates) prior to swimming helps to maintain constant blood sugar levels.
2. Foot care, cleanliness, and skin breakdown are monitored as they contribute to diabetes.
3. Access to privacy allows testing and administration of insulin.

Practical Applications
1. Weight control is managed with regular aerobic water activity.
2. Since activity levels affect insulin-sugar balance, staff are prepared to administer carbohydrate snacks when they observe one of the above mentioned characteristics.
3. Stroke adjustment is not necessarily needed; more time is devoted to stroke use than, for example, floatation, during each aquatic experience since this improves fitness.

Sensory and Communication Impairments
Hearing

Population Descriptors
A person who is deaf is unable, with or without a hearing aid, to process linguistic information while a person who is hard-of-hearing is able to process linguistic information with or without a hearing aid. A hearing loss of 70 dbs (decibels) in the better ear separates persons who are deaf from those who are hard-of-hearing. Loss prior to age three is considered a prelingual loss and affects language development. Characteristics evident with hearing loss include: Restlessness, shuffling gait, abnormal head tilts and rotations, balance disorders, and lowered fitness levels.

Swim Program Precautions
1. Hearing devices are worn either behind the ear, on the chest, or with eyeglasses; battery contact with water is to be avoided.
2. Establish a safety warning (visual) signal before instruction.
3. Participants might hesitate to submerge their faces so their eyes are below water as this is their communication medium.
4. Clearness of speech is critical; exaggeration of words as occurs when speaking louder is not necessarily helpful.
5. Various forms of communication are used: sign language, manual alphabet, manual writing, and combinations of speech reading and signing. Therefore, visual distance between the instructor and swimmer is considered as participants are taught.
6. Minimize glare on the water. Avoid having the participant look into the sun/bright light as instructions are given.
7. Water pressure is felt as the swimmer submerges so the swimmer may not appear apprehensive prior to a bob but upon recovery may exhibit fear.

Practical Applications
1. Demonstration, guided discovery, and modeling are used more than verbal communication.
2. Swimming fosters balance, endurance, relaxation, and proper body alignment.

3. Rotation from prone to supine or vertical to horizontal positions is practiced as balance deficits affect this action.

4. Bobbing helps breath control which aids relaxation.

5. Water walking, jogging, and lap swimming improve endurance while lessening restlessness and hyperactive behaviors.

6. Swimmers may exhibit gravitational insecurity and therefore require additional time developing buoyancy, for example, grasping sticks below the water surface and losing and regaining balance.

Visual

Population Descriptors
Persons are considered partially sighted or functionally blind if they can see no more at a distance of 20 feet away than what a person with normal vision can see at 70 feet (20/70 vision). The term blind is applied to persons with a visual acuity of 20/200 or less or whose visual field is limited to 20 degrees or less of the 180 degree field. Many persons with visual impairments perceive light or motion. Functional ability is most affected by age of onset and residual vision. Physical characteristics include: Blindisms (rocking back and forth or waving the fingers before the face), rigid posture with a tendency to lean forward, tendency toward lowered fitness levels and obesity, and perceptual-motor deficits.

Swim Program Precautions
1. Directional cues like relationship of objects to the numbers on the face of a clock or comparison of travel direction to letters of the alphabet and auditory cues like judging distance by vibration sounds help independent mobility. The swimmer might count the number of steps from end to end or the number of strokes from side to side.

2. Establishing an auditory warning cue prior to instruction helps independence and safety.

3. Submerging of the ears is initially avoided as this is the communication medium; this affects horizontal strokes and bobbing.

4. Describing the location of the person with a visual impairment to other persons/objects in the environment is necessary. Prior to entry, the swimmer moves around the perimeter of the water touching each piece of apparatus; once in the water, touching of objects is repeated.

5. Type of visual loss is identified prior to instruction so accommodations are appropriate. For example, peripheral vs tunnel vision requires different instructor positioning.

6. Minimize glare on the water. Avoid having the participant face the sun/bright light as instructions are given; shadows or uneven light are distracting.

Practical Applications
1. Tactile and auditory sensations are used with demonstration, guided discovery, and assistive devices like lane markers. The instructor describes the course of action prior to physically assisting the swimmer.

Instructor provides tactile orientation to child with visual impairment.

2. Independent mobility and fitness occur in swimming.

3. Water orientation includes time to adjust to water hitting the face.

4. Bobbing and underwater games help spacial awareness and depth perception. Even though the swimmer prefers the head above the water, bobbing is essential as other swimmers might splash a person who is blind not realizing the visual loss.

5. Allowing the participant to touch the instructor as a skill is demonstrated helps comprehension of how strokes are performed.

6. Bilateral movements with ears above the water, such as breaststroke, help water adjustment and are easier to coordinate than alternating strokes, the crawl, for example.

7. The instructor talks to the participant when the ears are out of the water.

8. A swimmer who is blind may choose to wear goggles because water may irritate the swimmer's eyes.

Emotional Impairments

Population Descriptors

Disorders are described by the American Psychiatric Association publication *Diagnostic and Statistical Manual of Mental Disorders* (DSM III revised, or most current edition). Stated criteria of medical diagnosis are presented by categories. A summary of relevant participant populations is presented:

Affective disorders describe mood impairments including manic and depressive syndromes. Manic episodes are characterized by hyperactivity, restlessness, talkativeness, distractibility, high-risk taking, and rapid speech activity. Depressive episodes are characterized by chronic fatigue, diminished interest, weight loss, inability to concentrate and make decisions, and lowered self-esteem.

Behavior and conduct disorders describe behaviors that fall outside the accepted realm and/or violate the basic rights of others and the norms and rules of society. These problems are repeated and persistent and include: Acting-out, aggression, withdrawal, running away, lack of guilt feelings, inability to show affection, manipulation, property damage, anxiety, fighting, profanity, and attention-seeking.

Personality disorders describe persons whose behaviors are so inflexible and maladaptive that their social and leisure functioning is impaired. Included are people who are eccentric, antisocial, and fearful or anxious, showing compulsive or passive-aggressive behaviors.

Psychoses describe persons who experience deviations in thought, perception, and affect to the extent that reality is tested. Persons distort reality through hallucinations and delusions; bizarre positions are assumed and ritualistic behaviors displayed, such as repeated entry-exit into pool or pacing in the changing area. Unusual fear of the water or perception of something in the water is possible.

Swim Program Precautions

1. Specialized interventions like behavior and crisis management procedures, desensitization, token economies, and challenge experiences affect staff management of participants during aquatics.

2. Medications in use have side effects like hyper- or hypoactivity and photosensitivity.

3. Interference during an out-of-control situation can be physically harmful; redirection is initially attempted and additional staff support is used.

4. Staff monitor participant goal setting as unrealistic expectations lead to further frustration, withdrawal, and anger.

5. Staff monitor participant's possessions and whereabouts as theft of items and running away happen.

6. Staff report inappropriate discussions like talk about suicide or crime to proper authorities.

7. Staff immediately define acceptable behavior like words and physical boundaries and consequences of noncompliance.

8. Staff are aware that they can become the objects of aggression or dislike meant for others so they learn to depersonalize feelings.

9. Management of each session is consistent, follows a routine, and includes immediate concrete reinforcement.

10. Behaviors like profanity or withdrawal are symptoms of underlying issues like substance abuse or neglect; staff report unusual physical signs like bruises or impulsive actions to the proper authorities.

Practical Applications

1. Touch and physical contact are used with discretion as they are interpreted differently by participants. The instructor may actually use an artificial device like a personal floatation vest so personal contact is avoided as the participant adjusts to swimming.

2. Orientation with slow gradual movements helps reduce tension and encourage relaxation; stretching and range of motion exercises accomplish this goal.

3. Control of environmental stimuli in the aquatic setting, like noise level, excess people, light reflection, or toys and devices in the water, supports adjustment and skill development. Attendance at a water park, for example, may be too stimulatory. The water itself is a cause of stimulation so when it is entered the swimmer is wrapped in a "stimulation blanket." If this occurs, the instructor gradually increases the amount of time in the water and entry into the water is very gradual; one limb at a time is introduced to the water. During adjustment to the water, the swimmer may be taken out of the water prior to "acting out" behaviors so control is regained.

4. Additional time is given to orientation and adjustment to the setting and the water environment as participants accept change with reluctance.

5. Bilateral movements, finning, sculling, and elementary back- and breaststrokes compensate for a lack of coordination.

6. Endurance is built with water walking, jogging, and lap swimming. Bobbing improves respiration. Use of kickboards and hand paddles improves strength.

7. Diving is a therapeutic tool as it provides risk and varying degrees of challenge; precision and accuracy, therefore, are sometimes de-emphasized.

8. To help participants attend and remain in control, instructors, for example, have small classes, require all participants except the one receiving instruction to remain at water's edge (briefly) until their turn, arrange class members so they do not touch each other, and keep the participants constantly in motion (one participant after the other swims a lap then all immediately return). Competition against others is discouraged; participants are rewarded for individual achievements.

9. Time between session activities is minimal; transition activities like individual contests are used.

10. Staff minimize words and rely on demonstration to teach skills; staff also avoid having participants be unsuccessful in front of others.

11. Buoyancy in the water may contribute to discomfort as the force of gravity felt as one stands on land is secure. Therefore, the swimmer may have to leave the water briefly to regain the feeling of security then return to feel the effects of buoyancy.

12. Pulling the swimmer (on his/her back) in an "S" design through the water helps the swimmer gain control over the defensiveness felt when positioned on the back.

13. Swimmers initially may not discern the difference between shallow and deep water; they may enter deep water without hesitancy or awareness of the dangers associated with not being able to stand on the bottom.

Social Impairments

Population Descriptors

Persons experience an array of nonspecific characteristics that affect their abilities to manage their personal lives and social relationships. Common characteristics of persons considered here and under "Addictions" are low self-esteem, social incompetence, limited resource acquisition skills, and feelings of entitlement.

Abuse and neglect affect children and adults and result from either physical, sexual, and/or emotional (mental) injury or negligent treatment (daily physical and mental needs are not met) that are harmful or threaten their health and welfare. Symptoms are nonspecific, meaning signs can be indicative of other unmet needs. Physical signs include bruises, burns, broken bones, brain damage, and poisoning. Emotional indicators are anxious or regressive behavior, depression, disinterest, distrust, isolation, and avoidance of intimate relationships.

Legal offenders have committed delinquent and criminal behaviors causing them to become involved with police, corrections, and/or the courts at either the national, state, and/or local level. Youth involved in unacceptable leisure behavior (gang behavior) commit delinquent acts, while adults who are frustrated, under extraordinary pressure, and/or perceive themselves as victims of unreasonable standards commit crimes. These persons are considered harmful to themselves and/or others. Other unresolved issues include lack of role models and family support, limited educational and financial skills and resources, personality disorders, mental retardation, suicidal behaviors, and sexual deviations.

Sexually transmitted diseases (STDs) are infections transmitted sexually or through contact with body fluids of a carrier. STD s include AIDS (acquired immunodeficiency syndrome) and HIV (human immune deficiency virus), chlamydia, gonorrhea, syphilis, HPV, warts, herpes, trichomoniasis, lice, and NSU (nonspecific urethritis). Death, cancer, and heart and reproductive problems result from these infections. Infection can remain asymptomatic and/or mask the presence of a second infection. Some symptoms include burning sensation upon urination, unusual discharge from the penis or vagina, lower abdominal pain, sores on the genitals and mouth, flu-like symptoms, fever, swollen lymph glands, head and muscle aches, and hair loss.

Swim Program Precautions

1. Requiring medical clearance/approval to use the aquatic environment informs staff that participation is not contraindicated to a swimmer's physical health.

2. Implementation of standard infection protocols on open wounds or cuts guards against spread of infection.

3. Securing of personal belongings as a routine procedure reduces vulnerability to loss or theft.

4. Staff discretion with touch and personal contact and defined procedures for documenting unusual physical, social, or emotional signs/behaviors are recommended.

5. Short-term or daily goals and rewards accommodate the unsure future of participants while compensating for their lowered self-esteems.

6. Media and research releases are emphasized to avoid either exploitation or exposure.

7. Staff comfort with behavior management strategies and crisis intervention protocols is helpful.

Practical Applications

1. Use games and sports to release energy (frustration) and develop acceptable social interaction skills. Emphasize target games rather than group competition where others can become unknowing targets for displaced aggressions.

2. Allow individual time so participants adapt to being with others and learn how to appropriately occupy their time.

3. Increase water adjustment time to accommodate unusual fears or previous lack of exposure to the aquatic setting.

4. Start with bilateral movements, elementary backstroke, and dog paddle, as participants might lack coordination.

5. Include family members or role models (big brothers/sisters) to give support and teach cooperative positive social interaction.

6. Avoid extended underwater periods initially as participants might be insecure not knowing what is happening above and around them.

7. Stretching exercises, range of motion activities, and breath control exercises encourage relaxation and develop endurance and strength.

8. Developing precision in the various strokes may not be as important as actual completion of the strokes.

9. Use of assistive devices might produce temporary secure feelings when the real need is to learn to trust one's own abilities and feel confident about what can be accomplished in the water.

10. Swimmers wearing clothing to cover their bodies do so to protect themselves from public embarrassment; privacy during changing is also important.

11. Like persons with emotional issues, persons experiencing social impairments do not accurately discriminate between a personally safe vs a dangerous situation. As a consequence, the swimmer approaches the water without attending to the potential hazards of the shallow vs deep water areas. Staff supervision is critical as is incorporating time into lessons to adjust to the various water depths.

Addictions

Population Descriptors

Eating disorders and substance dependence and abuse are described in the American Psychiatric Association publication *Diagnostic and Statistical Manual of Mental Disorders* (DSM III revised, or most current edition). These disorders are either primary disorders and/or are associated with contributory factors like HIV, homelessness, legal offenses, a dual-diagnosis like mental illness-chemical abuse, and emotional and social impairments with young adults.

Eating disorders are gross disturbances in eating behaviors. Anorexia nervosa is an extended period of not eating that can result in severe weight loss, starvation, and death; bulimia nervosa involves frequent overeating in massive quantities or constant eating followed by self-induced vomiting, use of laxatives or diuretics, fasting, compulsive exercise, and overconcern for body shape and weight. These diseases are chronic and progressive, not curable; persons learn to live in recovery. Other characteristics include isolation, mood swings, depression, fatigue, dizziness, blurred vision, headaches, memory loss, frustration, unrealistic expectations of self, high blood pressure, and increased cholesterol levels.

Psychoactive substance dependence and abuse describes a person who continues to use natural and/or synthetic chemicals and alcohol for nonmedical use despite adverse social, occupational, psychological, and physical conditions. Dependence is characterized by tolerance and withdrawal while abuse is more likely to be associated with recent consumption of, for example, alcohol, yet less likely to involve the above two behaviors. Each type of substance has different outcomes unique to each user yet the mind, emotions, and behaviors are effected. Withdrawal from use also has harmful effects like convulsions, tremors, disorientation, and anorexia. General effects are: Balance, coordination, and motor deficits; volatile emotions and mood swings; confusion, concentration, and memory deficits; and euphoria and impaired judgment.

Swim Program Precautions

1. Medical supervision and/or release is recommended.

2. Close supervision and monitoring of actual time in the water and physical exertion curtails compulsive overexercising.

3. Structure, routine, behavior management, relaxation, and reality orientation strategies are used to help participants set realistic expectations, decrease anxiety, and comply with staff rules and safety procedures.

4. Staff monitor areas where secret consumption occurs, such as the changing or entry areas.

Practical Applications

1. Staff are conscious to point out aquatic benefits (e.g., lower blood pressure rates and weight control) as related to wellness and needed lifestyle changes (appropriate use of leisure) yet realize that such changes take time and that persons with eating disorders are already extremely conscious of body-image.

2. Lowered physical fitness levels are improved with water walking, jogging, and aerobic exercises.

3. Respiratory capacity is enhanced with bobbing and breath control activities.

4. Water games (e.g., volleyball) require spontaneous actions which help participants relax and learn to have "fun."

5. Accuracy and perfection with stroke use are de-emphasized as participants tend either to be overly (eating disorders) or under (substance use) concerned about "how well they perform."

6. The need to achieve natural "highs" is met with diving and water park-type activities.

7. Staff create opportunities for participants to lead and/or demonstrate skills to aid in self-esteem building.

8. Cooperative group activities (e.g., circle routines) are used to help participants receive support and reinforcement. Class size is decreased/increased to accommodate recovery stage of participants (smaller size with inpatient than outpatient).

9. Participants' initial hesitations to back float or put their heads under water might relate to a lack of trust or secure feelings and/or newness of the setting.

10. Concluding the session with formal debriefings helps participants realize immediate benefits and provides opportunities for their input into future experiences; this helps self-determination.

11. Swimmers may choose to wear clothing to cover the effects of their addictions.

Management in the Aquatic Environment

In this concluding section, management of four areas is considered: Participants, personnel, instruction, and physical resources. The section focuses on service delivery in a safe aquatic environment and enhancement of participant access while in aquatic experiences. Risk management and accessibility materials are, therefore, incorporated throughout the section.

Covered in the first portion are participant concerns: Risk management, safety, particular illnesses/disabilities that affect participant well-being in the aquatic setting, participant assistance in the aquatic environment, and treatment precautions. Personnel information is presented in the second portion. Documents and procedures used during instruction are presented in the third portion of this section. Considered in the final segment are physical resources available in the aquatic environment. Facility accessibility and adapted equipment resources are presented.

PARTICIPANT CONCERNS

General Risk Management Guidelines

These guidelines suggest information to include in either the agency's risk management plan or a plan unique to the agency's aquatic program.

1. Participant registration includes background medical/health data, medications, safety precautions, behavioral concerns, emergency phone numbers, doctor information and summary of previous aquatic activities.

2. If seizure activity has ever occurred, record of the type, frequency, duration, date of most recent seizure, aura (warnings), postseizure behavior, medications, and dosage accompany registration information.

3. Participant confidentiality is considered yet staff have ready access to this information when the need arises.

4. Publicity on the program delineates its nature by describing participant skill prerequisites, expected behaviors and outcomes, staff to participant ratio, and participant management policies.

5. Information is managed so progress is routinely documented and reported to caregivers, participants, and future instructors.

6. Staff orientation and inservices are documented and include topics covered in this manual. This information is also made available to lifeguards and volunteers. Staff supervision ensures that techniques are properly implemented and participant responses accurately recorded. Staff credentials and supervisory records are maintained and readily available.

7. A plan of supervision is prepared to cover any participant activity in and around the aquatic area (entry-exit areas, dressing areas, deck/shore, and administrative locations).

8. Legal review and endorsement is secured for an emergency action plan including the documents used to report incidents and accidents.

9. An assessment process assures that each participant satisfies skill prerequisites before program entry. By completing assessments before instruction begins, staff also identify teaching methods and assistive devices to use during actual intervention.

10. Staff teach skills as they are presented in the skill progression and their documentation reflects participant acquisition of these skills.

11. Staff are assigned to work with participants according to the swimmer's needs. To illustrate, a tall participant is paired with an instructor who also is either tall or capable of physically handling the swimmer if safety demands.

12. Aquatic rules and procedures are posted and prior to instruction staff review them with participants. Lesson plans reflect this as part of each session. Likewise an orientation to the aquatic area precedes any instruction.

Safety

General safety precautions with persons with disabilities in the aquatic environment include the following:

1. Assist individuals with balance deficits during entry and exit, while walking on wet or slippery surfaces, and in the changing or locker room area.

2. Rather than carrying persons, use wheelchairs or modified deck chairs to move from the changing area to the water's edge. If lifting is necessary, a recommended approach is to have at least two or more persons present with each lifting no more than 1/4 to 1/3 of their respective body weights.

3. Alert lifeguards to persons with seizures and specific medical/safety concerns prior to entry into the water. Practice emergency care procedures and emergency water exits with swimmers present.

4. When participants roll to water's edge in wheelchairs, lock the chairs and assure that they will remain stationary as swimmers enter and exit the water.

5. Signage to inform of safety precautions may have little meaning to persons with cognitive disabilities. Persons with sensory and communication disabilities also may not be aware of water depth markings and boundaries. Prior to instruction make participants aware of warning devices like red and green lights at the shallow and deep ends, texture changes around the entry/exit areas and underwater surfaces, and lane markers and buoys floating in the water.

6. Before participants enter the water area, orient them to the area and review the rules. At water's edge affirm their awareness of rules and water depths. Identify locations of lifeguards, entry-exit points, and staff members.

7. Floatation devices are best used as teaching aids rather than as safety devices. Participants can not be assumed to be water safe just because they are wearing such devices.

8. When swimmers and the instructor are both in the water, the safest instructional formation is to have all of the participants in front of the instructor in a semi-circle formation.

9. Some swimmers may lack a preservation instinct and, consequently, be unaware of how to move to a safe depth when the water is over their heads. One approach is to set boundaries prior to instruction. Another is to instruct participants in how to move to water's edge and to develop a stroke which allows maintenance of regular breathing.

10. Participants may neither recognize the signs of fatigue nor realize how to cope with exhaustion. Periodic rest checks help monitor swimmer energy levels.

11. Water pressure around the chest area of persons with cardiac conditions may cause labored breathing. Also, very warm water may be contraindicated as blood pressure is increased.

12. Persons may be unaware of how water affects their functioning abilities and/or they may have inaccurate perceptions of their abilities. A recommendation is to test skills with initial water entry.

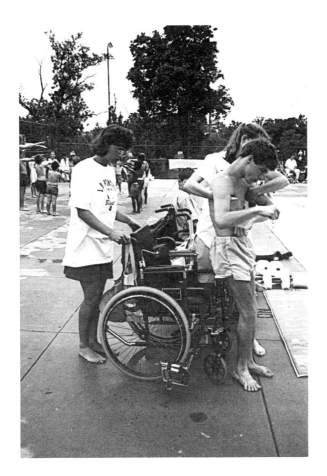

**Individual with balance deficits
and mobility impairment is
supported during water entry.**

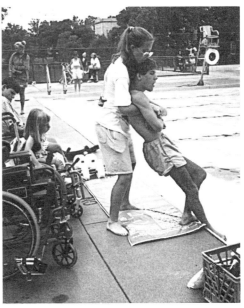

13. While observing participants, note breathing patterns especially for signs of hyperventilation. Also, note any excessive intake of water. Intervene if breath control is not evident.

14. With participants who are cognitively and emotionally impaired, a new or unfamiliar place may cause either an aggressive or withdrawal reaction. Set expectations and consequences prior to entry.

15. A participant's safety in water is best judged by analysis of skills achieved on the swim progression rather than by degree of independence on land.

16. Safety is assured by communication among staff in the water, at the water's edge, and in lifeguard positions. Training participants to respond to specific signals during each aquatic experience is a suggested safety practice.

17. Fear of the aquatic environment results from lack of previous experience in and around the water, newness or change of routine associated with emotional impairments, apprehension resulting from the impairment having happened in the aquatic environment, and an inability to comprehend the effects of water properties (buoyancy) on the participant (cognitive impairments). Water adjustment periods are extended and incorporated into each session to encourage trust between the instructor and participant and allow the participant to gain confidence.

Seizures

In an aquatic environment, there are several factors that may precipitate seizure activity:

Risk Factors	Precautions
Heat	Frequent intake of fluids Move out of the sun Enter water to cool off Stop with signs of nausea, blurred vision, dizziness Medical attention is needed with signs of heat stroke
Excitement	Avoid water attractions or areas causing fear/anxiety Relax away from activity Leave water if aura occurs Notify lifeguard/staff
Sun's rays/intensity	Move out of sun Avoid looking directly into sunlight Wear sun glasses Swim with companion
Medication	Take as prescribed Monitor activity level as exercise increases rate of absorption into the body Photosensitivity is a side effect of some medications so sun blocks are used
Alcohol	Mixed with activity may increase seizure activity so avoid before swimming

Managing a Seizure

Designing a safe environment

1. Remove physical objects in and surrounding the water area and in the changing areas that could injure swimmers if they were to fall, trip, and/or hit their heads.

2. Designate a specific area to store a mat or blanket used to lay a person on who has had a seizure. While in the water, move this to an accessible identified location near the water's edge.

3. Control of the temperatures and humidity levels in the aquatic environment and changing areas (86-90 degrees water temperature and 82-86 degrees air temperature) avoids extreme changes that precipitate seizure activity.

4. Staff observe the behavioral patterns of participants before, during, and after the aquatic experience to note an aura or seizure activity.

Using the aquatic environment

1. An appropriate staff/swimmer ratio is maintained during entrance and exit from the aquatic environment.

2. Participants wearing protective head gear, remove the gear after entering the water and replace the gear as they prepare to exit the water. While in the water, the gear is placed in an identified area near the water's edge.

3. Staff functions include:
   a. Maintain eye contact with assigned swimmers.
   b. Observe breathing patterns for hyperventilation.
   c. Note water temperatures, humidity (muggy conditions), and air temperatures for highs, lows, and changes.
   d. Observe changes in behavior or swim activity of assigned swimmers.
   e. Discriminate between a drop seizure and a prone float and/or bob. Drop seizures happen quickly and quietly.

Procedures to follow when a seizure occurs in the water

1. Petit mal (absence) and grand mal (tonic-clonic) seizures
   a. Raise the swimmer's head above the water and tilt it back to keep the airway clear. Keep the swimmer away from the wall.
   b. Look, listen, and feel for breathing. Mouth to mouth or mouth to nose resuscitation is given immediately.
   c. Talk calmly to reassure the swimmer.
   d. Time all seizure activity and record in appropriate documents.
2. Specific instructions with petit mal (absence) seizures
   a. Keep the swimmer in the water.
   b. After recovery, the swimmer may stay in the water, unless a second seizure is experienced.
   c. Wait for recovery; when the swimmer responds, assist with exit.
3. Specific instructions with grand mal (tonic-clonic) seizures
   a. Maintain the swimmer's head above the water throughout the seizure.
   b. Remove the swimmer from the water after the seizure is over.
   c. Place the swimmer on a mat on his/her side, check the airway and pulse.
   d. Check for ingestion of fluids as large quantities of fluids can restrict air flow and damage blood cells within 30–60 minutes.

Calling a life/rescue squad

1. Call as quickly as staff determines the need.
2. Tell them what you need, who you are, where you are (exact address), telephone number from which you are calling, directions to access water area, condition of swimmer; hang up last.
3. Organize swimmer's medical and emergency information.
4. Send someone to entrance to direct squad into area.
5. Notify proper administrative authorities and family.
6. Supervise other swimmers and/or redirect their attention if necessary.
7. Document the incident in appropriate record.

Hepatitis B

Hepatitis B is an inflammation of the liver caused by the hepatitis B virus. Persons who live in congregate housing settings, exhibit poor personal hygiene, and/or live in high risk situations (presence of substance abuse) experience higher probability of either having hepatitis or becoming carriers. In the aquatic setting, staff are exposed to the potential of infection or becoming carriers. Casual contact, coughing, sneezing, or contact with the urine and feces of infected persons does not spread the infection. When blood or bodily fluids containing blood penetrate the skin through scratches, infection may result. Persons with the infection or known to be carriers should not be permitted to swim when open cuts exist. If scratches occur during instruction, participants should exit the pool immediately and have the wound covered. Staff attending these participants should wear disposable gloves, wash any surface exposed to blood or body fluids with soap and water, and disinfect with a solution consisting of one cup of household bleach to one gallon of water. Neither participants nor staff should be permitted to share suits, towels, or other personal items on which blood and bodily fluids are transferred from one person to another. A preventative measure is to have participants and staff report their health status relative to hepatitis B on the medical entry forms.

Atlantoaxial Instability in Down Syndrome

Persons with Down Syndrome experience lax ligaments and apparent looseness of the joints which contribute to atlantoaxial instability. The muscles and ligaments around the joint of the two cervical vertebrae, the atlas and the axis, may be unstable, which permits the vertebrae to slip out of alignment resulting in symptoms of spinal cord compression. Paralysis could occur if participating in activities which either flex or hyperextend the neck. Evidence of instability is determined by x-ray. Participants may have x-ray evidence of instability yet show no symptoms. Participants with x-ray evidence of instability and symptoms may be prohibited from high-risk activities like the butterfly stroke, diving, and versions of water polo and rugby. Symptoms include: Increased clumsiness, walking fatigue, sudden preference for sitting, gait changes, bowel and bladder dysfunction, neck posturing changes and pain, limited neck motion, weakness in any extremity, spasticity, and hyperactive reflexes. Managers may choose to require an x-ray with medical recommendations (waiver and/or release from specific aquatic experiences) as participation prerequisites.

Assisting with Dressing, Lifts, and Transfers

For some individuals with physical disabilities, their ability to enter into an aquatic activity will depend upon some degree of personal assistance during preparation. The staff member's ability to assist the individual in an unobtrusive manner is an important factor in program inclusion. Several factors are considered prior to offering assistance:

1. Assess the participant's strengths and limitations, asking what can and can not be accomplished independently. Clarify precautions due to medical issues and assistive devices already in use.

2. Encourage the participant to complete as much of the task as possible without assistance; offer to help only when the participant can do no more comfortably and without frustration.

3. Explain prior to assisting what and how assistance will be given and what the participant is expected (capable) to do to help.

4. Determine the participant's readiness to begin/complete the task. Provide firm support (grasp, hold) using slow movements.

Dressing

The positioning of the participant during dressing will largely depend upon the participant's ability to assist during the process. Participants with sitting balance who are able to assist are best dressed from a seated position. Persons who need support while sitting or are unable to assist with dressing are best assisted from a lying position.

1. When removing clothing, encourage the participant to pull the arms (legs) from the garment as it is held. Participants with spasticity may require assistance to straighten the arm, hand, leg, foot. If so, move from the proximal to the distal or shoulder to hand and upper thigh to foot.

2. When dressing, place the clothing on the more physically involved arm or leg first. When undressing, take off clothes on the less physically involved arm or leg first. This allows the participant to use the less involved arm/leg to assist.

3. To avoid compromising the integrity and privacy of older participants, consideration is given to the gender of the assistant and the nature of the changing area, uni-sex bathroom, or segregated restrooms. A comfortable inclusive social situation may necessitate that the participant either come prepared to swim or wait until the area is available for exclusive use by the participant and assistant.

4. If dressing/undressing from a seated position with restraining/positioning straps present, complete the task prior to removing the straps so the participant's body alignment, safety, and positioning are assured.

5. When putting on/taking off pants for a participant in a seated position, stand behind the participant, keep the participant's shoulders forward by placing the assistant's arms under the participant's arms. Turn or rotate the body to one side, then the other to slide the pants on/off. To lift the participant, raise from the hips rather than with the arms.

6. For a pull-over garment, the participant leans forward slightly while the garment is pulled from back to front. The participant may hyperextend or become spastic (stiff) if the head is forced backward.

7. Flex the legs and feet prior to putting on socks and shoes. If the legs are straight, the participant is likely to become spastic (stiff). Roll rather than pull the socks onto the foot.

8. Place a rolled towel or pillow under the head and shoulders of a participant lying down to be dressed. This decreases the tendency to push backward which increases stiffness.

9. For persons with either hypertonic or spastic muscle tone, avoid pulling against spasticity, as this causes stiffness; avoid lifting by the arms, as this increases extension; and avoid moving quickly, as this causes the startle reflex.

Lifting and Transfers

The participant may be able either to complete part of the process or direct the assistant(s) during the lift/transfer. Plan the lift/transfer with the participant. If a lift requires more than one quarter of the staff member's body weight, additional assistance is suggested. Mechanical lifting devices promote independence, minimize physical effort, and are safer for both participant and assistant(s).

1. With a team lift, one staff member directs the actions and gives all verbal directions including the initial start command. This person is usually the one with whom the participant communicates or has eye contact.

2. Prior to a lift/transfer, confirm that the wheelchair brakes are properly locked. Clear the intended route of obstacles; be sure the footing surface is dry and that the least possible distance exists between the two transition points. Maintain the participant's safety straps until it is necessary to remove them so the lift/transfer happens.

3. During the move, the participant should be able to see the destination. Staff plan the move so medical needs are not compromised: Shunts, shoulder subluxation, flaccid muscle tone, decreased sensation, external collecting devices, and life support systems.

4. Move the participant toward the stronger side while providing assistance from the weaker side. This allows the participant to use the stronger side.

5. When the move is completed, confirm the participant is secure and positioned properly. Garments are arranged to avoid wrinkles/discomfort and straps are fastened. Personal assistive devices are properly placed/secured (lap boards, communication devices, etc.).

Chair lift facilitates water entry.
See also illustrations on pages 55 and 59.

Care of Assistive Devices

Wheelchairs

1. When assisting with wheelchairs, the safest pace is a walking gait with the assistant wearing tie shoes rather than rubber floppies or thongs that might lack traction on wet surfaces.

2. Brakes on stationary chairs should be locked. Unless near the edge of a dock, participant straps/restraints should be fastened. If near the dock edge, consideration is given to removing straps/restraints so if the chair were to roll into the water, the participant could be free of the weight of the chair.

3. If the entry to the waterfront area is down an incline, the assistant should turn the chair backwards and move toward the water so the participant's weight does not propel the chair toward the water. Steps are also done backwards so the participant does not fall forward.

4. Turnstiles and controlled entry areas into pools interfere with participant accessibility. Staff are cautioned as they maneuver through such areas to observe clearance of all chair parts and the participant's limbs.

5. Electric wheelchairs may require recharging while participants are swimming. The electric components should be protected from exposure to water.

6. Having extra transport chairs to use between changing and water areas protects the expensive sport chairs and chairs with padded or foam cushions.

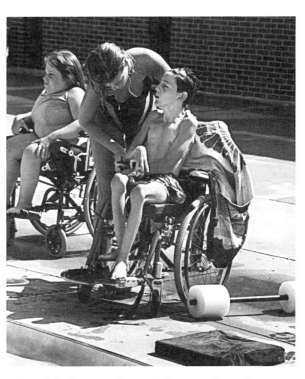

Wheelchairs need special attention when used in the aquatic environment.

Braces

1. Seek assistance from the participant as personal devices are taken off/on to ensure proper fitting and replacement.

2. Evidence of damage to the device or injury to the participant as changing occurs is reported as further use might be more harmful and create, for example, a bed sore.

3. Mud, sand, and water cause damage to devices and the participant if wet skin rubs against a brace, for example; thus, the device and participant are dried thoroughly.

Crutches

1. Damaged or worn rubber tips affect traction; thus, condition of tips is monitored and reported.

2. Friction between wet skin and a crutch can cause discomfort and reduce grip effectiveness; thus, drying before use is practiced (even temporarily between water's edge and changing area).

3. Staff transport between the changing area and water using specially designed aquatic chairs is a safe alternative to using crutches on wet/uneven surfaces.

Eye Glasses, Hearing Aids, Ear Tubes, Prostheses, Inhalers

1. The nature of the aquatic event and the participant's safety determine whether or not glasses remain on or are removed. If removed, this may occur immediately after entry with replacement prior to exit. If used, participants may elect to also wear retaining straps, caps, or protective goggles. Participants may elect to have a second pair to use in the water as chemicals corrode frames.

2. Hearing aids are usually removed and placed away from the water in protective cases so they do not become wet or affected by the humidity.

3. Individuals with tubes use ear molds to prevent water entry into the ears. Molds are either prescriptive or self-molded. If self-molded, staff periodically check to assure that they remain in the ear. Personalized molds are also checked yet are more likely to remain in place. Caps help keep molds in place. When swimmers submerge below three feet the water pressure might be painful.

4. Persons who wear prostheses may feel more comfortable changing in a private area and having larger than usual storage areas in which to place the prostheses.

5. Persons with asthma or other allergies who use inhalers while in the aquatic setting need quick access to them so portable protective coverings (plastic storage cases) are provided; they are well marked and placed near the water's edge.

Treatment Precautions

Administering Medications and Fluids

Fluids and medications are given through butterfly infusion needles and angiocath and heparin lock needles inserted into the veins. They are also given orally, rectally, by injection, and through naso-gastric tubes.

Recommendations
Administration by licensed health care professional.
Maintain record of dosage, when and how administered, special administration procedures, potential side effects, and preparation.
Plan for emergencies related to side effects and administration.
Plan for secure and appropriate storage.
Document any procedure related to medications/fluids.
Avoid sustained contact or pressure to site of device.
Cover with air-tight waterproof device.

Cast Care

Casts immobilize bones and joints to prevent or correct deformities. Limb mobility is limited by cast size and location.

Recommendations
Know type of cast, reason it is worn, positions needed due to cast, signs and symptoms of complications, and conditions that indicate cast is tight or rubbing.
Check skin condition regularly.
Check correct positioning regularly.
Document sign of poor circulation or skin breakdown.

Document any change in condition of cast.
Cover cast in air-tight waterproof device.
Avoid trauma to casted limb.
Add floatation device(s) to aid mobility, range of motion.

Catheterization

There are two types of drainage of urine from the bladder with insertion of a flexible tube: Indwelling catheters with external collection bag and clean intermittent catheterization.

Recommendations
Completed by qualified licensed health care professional or trained personnel.
Completed in private area with hand washing sink available.
Know signs and symptoms of urinary tract infections and problems.
Encourage fluid intake.
Maintain record of fluid intake, catheterization time(s), urine amount, and signs of infection.
Wear vinyl or latex gloves.
Follow specific schedule with intermittent catheterization.
When collection bag is worn, drain before and after swim and ensure seal of appliance is air-tight; secure pouch with rubber belt; during lifts and transfers avoid pressure on pouch.
Adjust bathing suit type to conceal pouch if worn.

G Tube (gastrostomy tube) and NG Tube (nasogastric tube)

A G tube is surgically placed into stomach to provide supplemental or total nutrition; NG tube is inserted into nose and leads to the stomach.

Recommendations
Know length of time after feeding before swimmer can be placed in supine position.
Document emergency procedures for tube blockage, displacement, formula rejection, and skin and stoma (opening) management.
Maintain record of physical reactions, amount of water given, signs that formula is not tolerated, signs of skin irritation around stoma or face.
Wear vinyl or latex gloves when having direct contact with tube.
Plug tube to prevent water entrance and avoid water entry into the nose that might cause a cough which could dislodge the tube.
Breath control portion of progression is not applicable.
Supine positions and strokes with therapist support recommended.

Ileostomy and Colostomy

Feces are eliminated through large intestine (colostomy) or small intestine (ileostomy) through stoma, into external collection device.

Recommendations
Know frequency of elimination, type of pouch used, procedures for changing pouch, and supplies needed to change pouch.
Design emergency plan to manage blockage of intestine causing cramps, dehydration from diarrhea, bleeding from stoma, and skin breakdown.

Document time of elimination, consistency of fecal matter, unusual discharge from stoma, skin irritations, and collection bag replacement.

Avoid trauma to clamp closing pouch and to pouch.

Provide private area to change/replace pouch.

Wear vinyl or latex gloves when changing pouch.

Empty pouch before and after swimming.

Adjust bathing suit style to conceal pouch.

Seal pouch closure so it is air-tight; secure pouch with rubber belt.

During lifts and transfers avoid pressure on stoma and pouch.

Tracheostomy and Suctioning

Tracheostomy is a surgical opening into trachea to allow breathing by use of a tube secured in place. Suctioning is needed when water enters tube or to remove mucus from tube, mouth, or back of throat.

Recommendations

Tube replacement or suctioning is completed by qualified health care or trained personnel.

Allow for rest period following suctioning; increased respiratory rate from exercise increases frequency of suctioning.

Know signs of respiratory distress: Bluish/grayish color of finger or toe nails, nasal flaring, mucus sounds in airway, increased heart rate, excessive choking, vomit, or aspiration.

Wear vinyl or latex gloves when suctioning or upon contact with mucus.

Document emergency procedures.

Know signs of need to suction: Nasal flaring, pale or bluish color around mouth, mucus bubbles at tube opening.

Prevent water from entering passage way; keep chest elevated.

Use supine strokes and positions with floatation devices.

When participant has no cough reflex, if water enters, suctioning must occur immediately.

Swimmer with tracheostomy needs to stay in water below shoulder level to protect surgical opening in neck.

Ventilator Dependent

Person receives breathing assistance through ventilator with tracheostomy tube. Amount of time on and off the ventilator varies with each person.

Recommendations

Training from qualified health care personnel to operate ventilator, position swimmer, and care for tracheostomy, suctioning, postural drainage, and communication.

Know how to manage power outages, respiratory distress, tube obstruction, tube displacement, infection or bleeding near tube or stoma and how to activate a mechanical ventilator.

Maintain record of emergencies including time mechanical ventilator is activated.

Prevent water or any item from obstructing tracheostomy.

Develop swimmer "help" signal.

Protect ventilator from water entry; use extra long air tube from ventilator to swimmer and prevent water from entering.

Use heavy duty grounded electrical cord from ventilator to electricity source.

Halo Vest and Collar

A halo stabilizes spinal column by immobilizing head and cervical spine. A collar stabilizes cervical column and prevents or reduces head movement.

Recommendations

Collar is changed if it becomes wet to prevent skin breakdown.

Aquatics limited to range of motion exercises, passive flexion and extension, water walking, vertical floating, breathing exercises with therapist support and neck and head above water.

Aquatic experience is therapeutic for individual on ventilator.

PERSONNEL INFORMATION

Sample job descriptions of staff who interact with persons with disabilities in the aquatic environment are contained in this section. These descriptions along with employee credentials, documentation of in-service training, supervision, and evaluation, and supportive information used during hiring and/or separation are maintained in employee files. Complete and updated files are kept as quality assurance measures.

Personnel assigned to each service level — therapeutic, adapted/specialized, and mainstreamed/integrated — have differing degrees of education, experience, and credential validation. Persons managing therapeutic programs are encouraged to have academic/medical preparation and credentials in professions servicing persons with disabilities along with appropriate specialty swimming instructor credentials and practical experience with the clientele served. For staff managing adapted/specialized programs, academic preparation or equivalent training with individuals with disabilities, swim instructor credentials, and aquatic experience with individuals with disabilities is recommended. Staff managing mainstreamed/integrated programs are encouraged to have previous training including information on individuals with disabilities and swim instructor credentials.

Descriptions cover general responsibility levels with aquatic programs. Functions are presented as guidelines rather than as performance-based standards as each manager develops expectations appropriate to the particular setting.

Aquatics Program Director

The director plans, organizes, conducts, and evaluates the aquatic program in accordance with the disabilities and skill levels of participants. This individual reports to a program manager and has as subordinates an assistant(s) and paid and/or volunteer instructional staff.

The director:

1. Assesses skills, safety/medical concerns, behavioral patterns, and supportive needs relative to the swim progression using pre-existing information, observation, and participant and/or guardian reporting.

2. Determines participant placement and groupings based on swim skills, safety/medical concerns, behaviors, support needs, and staff capabilities.

3. Assigns assistant director(s) to participant (group) according to the needs and assistant director(s) capabilities.

4. Adjusts placements (groups) and staff assignments as needed to allow for participant progressions and personnel changes.

5. Ensures participant, staff, and volunteer safety by following risk management and supervisory plan protocols and working closely with lifeguard(s).

6. Notifies guards of participant safety, medical and behavioral concerns, and staff changes; monitors their responsiveness to participants and staff.

7. Provides instruction and assistance to assistant director(s), staff, and volunteers as needed.

8. Evaluates assistant director(s), staff, and volunteers and identifies inservice training needs.

9. Reports to program manager the program needs and concerns relative to facility, participants, staff, volunteers, equipment, and supplies.

10. Completes reports and records and submits to program manager.

11. Oversees completion of paperwork requirements by assistant director(s), staff, and volunteers.

12. Maintains current medical/safety information on all participants through ongoing communication with participant/guardian and agency personnel. Reviews information regularly with assistant director(s) to ensure record updating.

13. Ensures safe and proper use and storage of equipment and security of facility.

14. Organizes and conducts formal program planning and evaluation sessions. Solicits and records input from staff and volunteers. Makes recommendations for future programs.

Aquatics Assistant Program Director

The assistant director is under the supervision of the aquatics program director and assumes the director's duties in the director's absence or when directed to do so. The person focuses on the needs of the participants as the program operates and helps staff with specific participant aquatic and management needs.

The assistant director:

1. Assists with program set-up and preparation of the changing and swimming areas to accommodate participant needs.

2. Meets with aquatics director to discuss/review staff-participant assignments and planned activities.

3. Reviews participant information and records in order to accurately interpret participant needs to staff.

4. Assists aquatics director with preparing staff and/or volunteers to carry out the day's lesson and individual program plans.

5. Observes staff and participants as program operates. Makes staff and participant shifts to meet needs.

6. Assists staff and participants in preparation for and following swimming. Monitors safety of staff and participants upon arrival/departure, during changing, and in the aquatic area.

7. Assists staff and/or volunteers during swim session with particular skills, medical/safety concerns, behaviors, and support needs.

8. Assists lifeguard(s) if called upon to do so.

9. Assists with facility and equipment clean-up and storage, safety and security checks, and completion of swim reports and records.

10. Assists staff and/or volunteers with session evaluation and preparation for next program. Reviews participant progress and reports to aquatics director. Reports staff needs to director.

11. Assists with maintaining up-to-date emergency information and reviews this information regularly with staff and/or volunteers.

Pool Manager/Lifeguard

The pool manager/lifeguard is ultimately responsible for the safety of swimmers, staff, and volunteers. The guard, who may or may not be familiar with individual swimmers, directs staff in what precautions to take when safety issues arise. Staff are responsible for assuring that participants comply with posted rules and guard requests. Guards assist staff when, for example, several participants are entering or exiting from limited access areas or staff request assistance to handle medical/behavioral emergencies.

The pool manager/lifeguard:

1. Brings to the director's attention any safety concerns.

2. Oversees and/or completes maintenance of changing and aquatics areas, water temperature, chemical balance, water clarity, and air temperature.

3. Reports any deviations to established standards and initiates corrective actions.

4. Maintains supplies adequate to ensure water quality and quality and safety of the swimming and changing areas.

5. Prepares and maintains preventative and routine maintenance schedules for the aquatic facility/area.

6. Prepares and maintains inventory of aquatic equipment and supplies.

7. Keeps logs and records of readings, temperatures, and adjustments made to meet specified standards.

8. Monitors and collects sign-in/sign-out sheets of aquatic staff.

9. Ensures facility and storage areas are properly secured.

10. Participates in aquatic planning and evaluation sessions. Recommends adjustments related to safety concerns and swimmer needs.

11. Remains knowledgeable of the required operating standards and codes affecting aquatic programs/facilities.

12. Retains and updates aquatic staff credential files.

13. Conducts aquatic staff and program staff and/or volunteer training on aquatic operations and procedures.

14. Prepares and files records/reports as necessary.

15. Supervises staff and participant actions during programs. Enforces rules and standards.

Staff and Volunteers

Staff report to assistant program and/or program directors. Primary responsibility is to instruct and supervise participants. This may also involve care and use of assistive and adaptive devices. Staff notify the lifeguard of participant safety issues as they arise. Staff supervise and assist volunteers during individual instruction. Volunteers are assigned to staff on site so if questions arise, response is immediate.

A staff member and/or volunteer:

1. Arrives prior to program so time is allowed to review individual participant aquatic information.

2. Notifies the supervisor of personal needs/abilities like use of ear plugs and preference to work with participants only in shallow water.

3. Assists participants in changing areas with personal needs. Ensures safety of participants as water entry/exit occurs.

4. Assists with aquatic area set-up/close-down and clean-up. Stores equipment, reports lost/found items, and records safety issues.

5. Remains with and monitors behavior of assigned participant for the duration of the program. Observes signs indicating health/safety/medical concerns and takes corrective action.

6. Uses the skill progression and daily lesson plan to guide session instruction. Verifies participant competence with program director prior to adjusting instruction.

7. Completes assessments/evaluations before and after sessions.

8. Notifies program director if unable to attend/volunteer for assigned program.

9. Respects confidential participant information. Supports participant autonomy. Respects participant dignity/privacy.

10. Reports expressed interests of participants/caregivers so information sheets are properly updated. Records any program adjustments/deviations to planned instruction.

11. Responds to lifeguard directives.

12. Practices aquatic safety behaviors. Complies with rules and regulations of site.

13. Marks/identifies unmarked possessions of participants.

14. Supervises participant interactions and group behaviors.

15. Motivates/disciplines participants as needed.

**Staff credentials and training determine aquatic assignments,
which are outlined in the plan of supervision,
along with staff to swimmer ratios.**

INSTRUCTION INFORMATION

Each swim session is organized using a lesson plan form (refer to page 39). Following each session, a written evaluation reports the activities, participant reactions, progress along the skill continuum, and resource use during the session. A plan of supervision guides the instruction and the evaluation. The plan is intended to reduce the risks to participants and staff during the session. The program director is responsible for ensuring that each session conforms to the recommendations of this plan.

If an incident or situation arises prior to, during, and/or following the session, the director collects facts to account for the behaviors and actions of involved persons. If an accident does occur, the director is also responsible to report the facts surrounding the event. Sample documents to use as sessions are conducted, evaluated, and managed are presented on the following pages.

Plan of Supervision—Swim Lesson

1. Upon arrival at the aquatic site, check safety of equipment, swim area, locker/restrooms, and entry-exit areas.

2. Review participant assignments with staff, including ADL needs and physical assistance needs during entry-exit.

3. Verify water quality, chemical levels, air and room temperatures, humidity readings, and anticipated weather conditions (outside area).

4. Place instructional and personal assistance equipment at needed sites. Secure items that need to be out of reach or might distract participants.

5. Review class management procedures and emergency protocol. Review information on each participant to affirm skill level, session goals, recommended interaction techniques, and related helpful hints. Practice emergency procedures, ensure phone/radio access.

6. Review lesson plans, determine instructional sites, and assign staff to participants.

7. As participants enter the aquatic area, review safety precautions and rules/regulations with swimmers. Observe the physical condition of swimmers and their responsiveness to staff instructions. Note personal swimmer items, mark if appropriate, and organize so swimmers are aware of where their belongings are kept.

8. Notify the lifeguards of needs such as seizures, photosensitivity, unusual fears or mannerisms, cardiac conditions, tactile defensiveness, and visual or hearing impairments. Plan to adapt emergency plans to accommodate these needs.

9. During instruction, staff on deck scan the water, listen for noise level changes and observe participant hypo or hyperactivity, proper use of personal assistive devices and instructional aids, participant compliance with staff requests, staff management of participant behaviors, any unusual condition surrounding the aquatic area, and lifeguard actions.

10. Monitor pool entry and exit. Ensure that swimmers are covered quickly if water/air temperatures are dissimilar. Supervise transfers, lifts, carries, and use of hydraulic equipment to ensure neither participants nor staff slip when wet meets dry. Swimming uses up participant energy so additional assistance to the locker/restroom areas might be needed following the lesson.

11. Ensure all participants and staff are clear of the swim area before the guards leave their stations. A supervisor monitors the aquatic area until all staff and swimmers are outside of the actual swimming area and the swimming area is secured.

12. Evaluations are completed after swimmers are comfortable and staff have checked their physical conditions and personal needs. Staff and participant comments are recorded. Status on the progression is noted. Any helpful teaching hints used during the session are recorded.

13. Equipment is checked and stored. Reports document water conditions, resource use, and necessary equipment repairs, replacements, and/or requests.

14. Reports are stored and the aquatic area is secured after all swimmers have safely left the aquatic area.

Critical Incident Report

A critical report form is used to report incidents that could lead to risk/safety of participants, staff, resources. If there is injury, an accident report form is also filled out. The form is reviewed by the supervisor and filed with risk management staff and/or the agency safety committee.

Program: Name_____Location_____

Participant (s) Name:_____Date & time _____

   Staff involved:_____

Nature of the incident

_____Physical abuse of self

_____Physical abuse of other participants

_____Physical abuse of staff

_____Physical aggression among participants

_____Physical aggression among participants and staff

_____Verbal abuse toward other participants

_____Verbal abuse toward staff

_____Destruction of equipment, property

_____Vacating program area unattended

_____Unsafe use of equipment, resources

_____Elopement (running away)

_____Noncompliance with staff policies or aquatic rules/regulations

_____Health or medical condition—explain_____

_____Other—explain_____

Antecedents: Explain the setting and interactions prior to the incident: _____

_____

Describe the incident from participant's viewpoint:_____

_____

Describe staff (and any other person's) intervention — what was done during and to control the
   incident: _____

_____

Immediate and long-term resolutions — what was done immediately following the incident and
   what will be done in the future:_____

_____

Who was notified?

_____Program supervisor

_____Parents/guardians

_____Police

_____Emergency squad

_____Other—explain_____

Signatures: Reporter_____

Witnesses: Name (s)_____Address_____

                                 _____Address_____

Supervisor (risk management officer): Name_____

                                   Date_____

Disposition by risk manager/safety committee:_____

_____ Date_____

Accident Report

An accident report is completed and accompanies the incident report if participants, staff, and/or volunteers are injured pre-, during, or post-program. The report is completed in ink, signed by the appropriate supervisors and witnesses, and filed according to the risk management protocol of the agency. One form is used with each injured person.

Program: Name_____Location_____

Injured person:Name_____Age_____Sex_____

        Address_____Phone_____

Date of injury:_____Time(am/pm)_____

Body part injured:_____

Type of injury :_____

Exact physical location of accident:_____

Explain how and what was observed to have caused the injury:_____

_____

_____

Action Taken:

_____Person requested no assistance

_____Person/staff requested first aid—who?_____

_____First aid given—explain what and by whom_____

_____

_____Notified program supervisor

_____Notified parents/guardians

_____Notified police

_____Notified emergency squad

_____Other—explain_____

_____Who made call(s)?_____

_____Who responded to call(s)?_____

_____Injured taken to place/doctor by whom?_____

Signatures: Reporter _____

Witnesses: Name(s)_____Address_____

        _____Address_____

Supervisor: Name_____Date_____

Follow-up: Date_____Who?_____

Notes or remarks:_____

_____

Disposition by risk management/safety committee:_____

_____Date_____

PHYSICAL RESOURCES

In this concluding portion of Section Three, physical resource management concerns are reviewed. General accessibility guidelines and equipment adaptations are presented. The intent is to present resource ideas appropriate in the aquatic environment with all persons including those with temporary and permanent illnesses and disabilities. The functioning ability of the participant relative to safety and swim skill acquisition influences physical resource modifications. Adjustments in resources, policies, personnel, and program content are warranted when participants would be better able to safely achieve skills on the swim progression if the changes were made. Such changes also meet the intent of ADA.

Adaptations made for one person do not always help another, the process is individualized. To illustrate, the installation of beepers or visual markers to assist persons with hearing or visual limitations distract persons who are unable to ignore their presence (e.g., attention deficit disorder children). The manager implements modification strategies that consider each individual as well as the nature of the groups using the aquatic facility.

Selecting and Designing an Aquatic Facility

The aquatic environment may refer to a variety of bodies of water including swimming pools, ponds, lakes, rivers, and oceans. For the purpose of teaching swimming to individuals with disabilities, swimming pools provide the most consistent environment conducive to skill development. Swimming pools vary in size and shape; most community pools designed to be multi-use facilities have a variety of depths while pools in clinical facilities tend to be singular-use with one depth. Multi-use pools usually have a shallow water instructional area, an area separated for competition and lane swimming, and a deep area with diving boards.

Pools designed for use by individuals with disabilities have built-in accessibility features. Multi-use pools are made more accessible with the addition of mechanical lifts and other access enhancing features. Accessibility requirements are specified in the *Americans with Disabilities Act Accessibility Guidelines for Buildings and Facilities* (ADAAG). ADAAG specifies criteria for parking areas, building entrances, shower rooms, and restrooms. Beyond these standards, accessibility is dependent upon individual user needs. Persons with dual diagnoses and/or multiple impairments develop skill in an aquatic setting with consistent depths and warm water while persons with fewer impairments acquire skills in a variety of settings. Aquatic facility considerations encompass several areas.

Facility Location

Is the facility centrally located and in an area where swimmers feel safe? What is the travel route, is the travel path accessible, and is travel assistance available (transport, handrails, auditory/visual guide markers)?

Parking Areas/Facility Entrance

Compliance with ADAAG criteria include the following:

Paved, level parking area having minimal slope, located adjacent to aquatic facility with required number of accessible parking spaces (facilities that specialize in treatment or services for persons with mobility impairments are to have 20% of the total number of parking spaces provided accessible).

Access aisle from accessible parking spaces directly to accessible entrance, most direct route without having to pass behind parked cars.

Accessible parking spaces clearly indicated with signs that are not hidden by parked vehicles.

Van accessible parking spaces with width allowing lift use (96 in. minimum).

A desirable feature is a covered passenger loading zone that includes an access aisle and ramp if there is a curb between the access aisle and the vehicle pull-up.

With evening programming, parking lot lighting is an important feature.

Accessible entrance is clearly marked; nonaccessible entrances direct individuals to the accessible entrance.

Shape of the door handles permits grasping with one hand; automatic or power assisted doors are desirable if facility is used heavily by individuals with disabilities.

Accessible entrance leads directly to the aquatic area including lockers, showers, restrooms, and change areas.

Aquatic office is located near accessible entrance so staff monitor arrivals, departures, information, and safety.

Locker Rooms/Restrooms/Shower Rooms

Design encourages independence before and after the swim experience and complies with ADAAG standards.

Five percent of toilets, sinks, and bathing units for the facility must meet ADAAG criteria.

If lockers are present, lower level lockers are available to persons using wheelchairs.

When benches are affixed to the floor, 36 in. space separates the benches from the lockers.

If wall-mounted hair dryers are provided, they are 46 to 54 in. high. Electrical outlets are provided for personal hand-held hair dryers. Ground-fault interrupters are installed with all electrical outlets.

Changing tables provide for assisted dressing. Extra beach-type shower chairs help during transfers.

Wall mounted towel hooks are provided at variable heights.

Nonslip floors throughout entire area are a safety feature.

Handrails are on walls throughout area.

An assisted dressing area permits a caregiver of opposite sex to be with the swimmer when this would otherwise be uncomfortable not only to the swimmer and caregiver but other users.

Controlled shower water temperatures ensure that users who lack sensation are not burned. Ideally the water turns on and off automatically; if not, several on-off control options exist.

Access from the locker area to the aquatic area is enhanced by being on the same level, having controlled heat and air temperatures, and having the required personal cleansing area as close as possible to the actual water area.

Pool Deck Area

ADAAG mandates program access and provides criteria for pool support areas yet does not list specific swimming pool standards. Desirable features include:

The ideal deck is even with the water level but no more than 12 in. above the water line and does not slope toward the water.

A nonslip deck is wide enough to allow three persons in separate wheelchairs to pass side by side.

Deck size accommodates entry and exit of more than one user group at a time and allows persons to wait without interrupting the aquatic experience of others.

Handrails attached to a wall or placed along the deck assist swimmers as they transition into the water.

Signage identifies depths, safety features, entry-exits, and "pool closed—no guard on duty"; persons with communication impairments are able to interpret this information.

Benches and accessible water fountains support independence.

Telephone, emergency numbers, and posted emergency procedures are usable by persons with cognitive and communication impairments.

A protected bulletin board/message board supports instruction.

Ideal deck area is uncluttered; allows quick access to storage areas for floatation devices, personal assistive devices, and portable transfer devices; and contains hooks to allow for drying towels and assistive devices. A shaded, protected deck area away from the water's edge to store user chairs while swimmers are in the water is helpful.

Water Entry-Exit Systems

Traditional pools present entry-exit difficulties to persons with physical impairments due to features like the height difference between the deck and water surface, ladders that have narrow rungs and wide spacing between the rungs, and vertical ladder entry into the water that causes refractive errors affecting persons with perceptual deficits.

Newer pools incorporate design features to enhance entry-exit. Included are movable floor systems that elevate the pool floor to the deck level, zero-depth entries, and construction of the deck to coincide with the water surface. A common feature of therapeutic pools is permanent ramps. Swimmers transfer to special pool chairs or remain in their personal chairs and roll into the water assisted by handrails. A dry ramp is an exterior ramp that allows the user to move to water surface level without having the chair enter the water.

When facility design does not incorporate accessibility features, a number of options exist to enhance entry-exit. Persons who experience balance and mobility impairments gain access by using portable pool steps. These steps are made of fiber glass or stainless steel to withstand the pool environment; they consume three to four feet of pool space in the shallow end, are removed when not in use, and have handrails, a nonslip surface, and enlarged steps (6-in. risers with 18-in. step/tread).

Persons in wheelchairs gain pool entry-exit using chair lifts. These lifts are mounted at pool side in the shallow end. They allow users to transfer from personal chairs to the pool lift chair with minimal assistance, operate on a hydraulic system so the amount of weight transferred is not an issue, and are removed and stored when not in use. Portable ramps are also available, but due to the slope required to gain access, the length of the ramps requires extensive pool space and larger amounts of storage space than other accessibility options. Persons in wheelchairs with upper arm strength use transfer steps; they transfer to a platform then down a few steps to the deck and pool.

Additional Entry-Exit Considerations

Pools are used by individuals with a variety of impairments, all of which are considered when entry-exit alternatives are planned.

Independence is increased with minimal mechanical or manual assistance.

Alternative entry-exit devices consume varying amounts of deck and pool space, which is considered as options are planned. Of special concern is the safety of the device as it relates to the swimmer's use of the pool, deck, and locker rooms. Also considered is the attachment of the device to the deck and the compatibility of this to the gutter system. Nonelectrical systems are recommended.

Storage is a consideration as is the ease with which the device is transferred from storage to pool side and installed.

Materials with which the device is constructed (noncorrosive) and the repair, part replacement, and maintenance are considered when selecting devices.

Pool Design, Depth, Dimensions

Instructional pools dedicate two-thirds of the total pool space to depths of four feet or less. A slope of no more than one inch in 18 inches with the deep end having a constant depth is preferred. A slip-resistant surface is desirable. The bottom is raised to decrease pool depth with the use of submerged platforms/chairs and hydraulic or movable floor systems. Therapy pools are generally smaller than instructional pools (20 by 40 feet with shallow water depth of three and one-half to five feet) and have handrails around the perimeters to grasp as water exercises are completed, for example.

Darkly painted objects on the bottom like lane markings hinder depth perception and if possible are to be avoided. Lane markings and warning and directional signage of highly contrasting colors are more visible to swimmers. Float dividers that mark increasing water depths are risk management tools.

Water Temperature

Water temperature gives a therapeutic effect to the aquatic experience as elevated temperatures permit muscle relaxation with individuals who experience spasticity, cerebral palsy, neuromuscular, and musculoskeletal impairments. With multi-use pools, temperatures elevated to over 80 degrees are uncomfortable for lap swimmers and competitive swimmers yet persons with physical impairments are uncomfortable with temperatures lower than 85 degrees.

Water temperature in therapeutic pools ranges from 92 to 98 degrees. This range provides neutral warmth (body temperature range) yet does contribute to fatigue and is therefore considered when planning length of time in the water. The maintenance of a temperature of 90 degrees or higher may result in a different pool classification (spa) and as such may require operation under different guidelines according to some state laws.

Water temperatures between 86 and 90 degrees are comfortable with most instructional swimmers as they are able to concentrate on the lesson and remain in the water long enough to practice their skills. When the pool is a multi-use pool, scheduling of lessons and user groups is coordinated with raising and lowering of the water temperature.

Air Temperature/Dehumidification Systems

Elevated water temperatures impact negatively the indoor aquatic environment. Excessive humidity created by evaporation from the warm water causing condensation contributes to corrosion, which is exacerbated by pool chemicals. Capacity to reduce the indoor humidity level is desirable and is accomplished in several ways. The pool enclosure is purged by introducing large quantities of dry

**Multi-use pool with shallow instructional area
separated from deep water diving area.**

outside air to replace humid inside air. Dehumidification systems extract moisture from the air and return dryer air to the pool environment. These systems are usually more expensive than systems that introduce outside air yet over a long period of time money is saved as they are more energy efficient. Additionally, the introduction of outside air creates a chilling effect on swimmers attributed to air velocity; less than 25 feet per minute (fpm) is recommended. A third alternative to control condensation and reduce humidity is a pool blanket placed on top of the water when the pool is not in use; heating costs are also reduced as heat loss through evaporation is reduced.

Specifications related to air temperature include:

Air temperature two degrees above pool water temperature is desirable as evaporation is controlled with this ratio.

Relative humidity, level of water vapor in the air, of 50 to 60% minimizes condensation and resulting corrosion.

Air velocity greater than 25 fpm creates a draft that chills swimmers.

State health codes address ventilation systems so options may vary from state to state. The desire is to introduce dry outside or filtered air to eliminate corrosive condensation.

Water Chemistry

Regulating the chemical balance of the pool water with individuals with disabilities has added dimensions. Warmer water temperatures increase the rate of evaporation and place greater demand on the chemical monitoring system. The possibility of incontinence and the use of collection devices expose the water to higher probability of foreign matter affecting chemical balance. Additionally, swimmers on various medications and those who may rub and/or keep their eyes open are sensitive to chemicals. Thus, when chemical levels are altered to compensate for one concern, another issue can be affected. A number of alternatives exist to the use of chlorine systems, such as bromine, the benefits of which are assessed as programs and services are planned.

Pool Lighting

The objective of indoor pool lighting is to maximize visibility throughout the facility while minimizing the effects of refraction. Depth perception is, therefore, enhanced with proper lighting.

Refraction is affected by lighting.
It is an important consideration for many individuals with disabilities.

Sufficient overhead and underwater lighting encourages movement exploration. Lighting that reveals the true flesh color of participants allows warning signs like bluish skin to be more easily detected.

Pool Acoustics

Concrete walls and ceilings create an echo elevating the noise level in a facility. This effect impacts instruction with swimmers having communication impairments and those who are distracted by additional stimuli (persons with autism); their response may be unacceptable and/or unsafe behaviors. A calm, quiet atmosphere is conducive to instruction. Limiting the class size might be necessary if acoustics contribute to a high noise level. Acoustical panels are commercially available and do eliminate excess noise.

Instructional Equipment

Swim equipment is used to support instruction and enhance learning. Swim equipment used with individuals with disabilities is similar to that used with other swimmers. The intent is to enhance independence. Use of specific equipment is presented here by its instructional intent.

Goal—Water Adjustment

Swim goggles, ear molds, swim caps, and nose clips promote comfort and may be used on a continuous basis. Goggles with adjustable straps and nose bridge, clear lens, leak proof eye pieces, and hypo-allergenic materials are used. Custom-made ear molds are prepared from silicone putty and are kept in place by a lycra swim cap. Nose clips are used with swimmers experiencing breath control difficulties like individuals with cerebral palsy.

During water adjustment, swimmers participate in exploratory activities using diving sticks, hula hoops, and objects that submerge to various water depths. Diving sticks stand vertically in the water and require the swimmer to bend at the waist and reach down to retrieve them; this promotes a horizontal position in the water that is needed to overcome gravitational insecurity. A hula hoop partially submerged in the water requires the swimmer to move in a horizontal position so spacial awareness is developed.

Goal—Floatation

The personal floatation device (PFD) is used primarily as a safety device. When a PFD is worn, instruction on proper use is given. Various floatation devices are used to facilitate a minimal degree of buoyancy in a horizontal position. Placement of the device is dependent on the swimmer's weight distribution and functioning abilities. Commonly they are worn on the back or stomach to enable body alignment needed to sustain a float and propel without interfering with arm and leg strokes.

Goal—Propulsion

A variety of devices are available to enable kicking and pulling. Kick training devices include kickboards, fins, bar bell floats, and hand-held floats (including milk or bleach bottles). Proper selection is dependent upon the swimmer's ability to grip the device and keep the arms extended. The bar bell is sometimes preferred over the kickboard as it is easier to grasp the bar bell than to pinch the kickboard. While some devices add stabilization, they inhibit a roll used in breathing; the bar bell best illustrates this concern so it is used to practice lifting the head to breathe while the kickboard is used to practice the head roll.

Fins create a larger kicking surface so they add thrust to the swimmer's natural kick. Swim fins also increase resistance to the up and down movement of the leg so strength is improved. Swim fins vary in length and flexibility; these qualities are important to consider when making purchases.

Pulling during propulsion is enhanced with hand paddles and swim gloves, used also to correct hand positioning. These devices help the instructor identify hand entry errors and stroke faults. Strength is also developed as resistance is increased; however, this increased resistance can cause shoulder injury and use of these devices is preferred only with advanced swimmers.

Masks and snorkels are used during propulsion. Swimming in a prone position without having to rotate, lift, or roll to breathe is the primary reason for their use. The swimmer needs to be able to expel water that accumulates inside the snorkel; development of sufficient lung capacity is important. Care and fitting of the mask, like goggles, is important to ensure swimmer comfort.

Goal—Safety

Swimmers become aware of proper use of emergency equipment like the backboard, ring buoy/torpedo, and shepherd's crook during orientation to the setting. Practice permits staff and swimmers to become aware of adjustments necessary to enable use with swimmers with disabilities. This practice helps swimmers become more comfortable with the devices and reasons for their use.

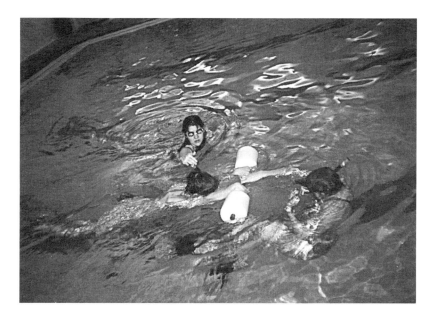

A variety of devices can help develop kicking and pulling skills. These swimmers are using bar bell floats. They are also using snorkels to aid in breath control.

APPENDIX

Sample Recording Forms

Division of Therapeutic Recreation
Information Form

This information form must be completed in full prior to participation in the therapeutic recreation programs. Please provide as much information as possible and return to: Cincinnati Recreation Commission, Division of Therapeutic Recreation, Centennial Two, 805 Central Ave., Cincinnati, OH 45202.

I. PARTICIPANT INFORMATION

First Name ☐☐☐☐☐☐☐☐☐   Last Name ☐☐☐☐☐☐☐☐☐☐☐☐☐☐

Address Number ☐☐☐☐☐   Street ☐☐☐☐☐☐☐☐☐☐☐☐☐☐☐☐

City ☐☐☐☐☐☐☐   Zip ☐☐☐☐☐   Home Phone ☐☐☐☐☐☐☐☐☐

Emergency Name ☐☐☐☐☐☐☐☐☐☐☐☐☐☐☐   Phone ☐☐☐☐☐☐☐☐☐

Mother's Work Phone ☐☐☐☐☐☐☐☐   Father's Work Phone ☐☐☐☐☐☐☐☐

Sex ☐   Date of Birth ☐☐ ☐☐ ☐☐
                         Month Day Year

Doctor's Name _____
Phone _____

School _____   Teacher Name _____

Group Home Agency _____   Agency Contact Name/Phone _____

II. DISABLING CONDITION

Please identify the participant's disabling condition. Circle all that apply to the participant and/or write in any disabling condition not listed.

Autism	Cerebral Palsy
Down Syndrome	Spina Bifida
Severe Mental Retardation	Spinal Cord Injury
Moderate Mental Retardation	Muscular Dystrophy
Mild Mental Retardation	Multiple Sclerosis
Learning Disability	Head Injury
Attention Deficit Disorder	Vision Impaired
Severe Behavior Disorder	Hearing Impaired
Emotional Disorder	Stroke
Other:	

Continued

Does participant walk independently? Yes___No___If no, what type of assistance is required? wheelchair___walker___other (please specify)

Does participant dress independently? Yes___No___If no, what assistance is needed?

Does participant bathroom/toilet independently? Yes___No___If no, what assistance is needed?

Does participant need assistance with catheterization? Yes___No___

Does participant communicate through speech? Yes___No___If no, what type of communication is used?

III. MEDICAL INFORMATION

Please circle all that apply to participant.

Allergies (specify below)	Glasses	Seizures
Arthritis	Hearing Aid	Shunt
Atlantoaxial Subluxation	Heart Condition	Tracheotomy
Catheter	Hepatitis Carrier	Other:
Diabetes	High Blood Pressure	
Diet Restriction	Respiratory Ailment	
Ear Tubes	Scoliosis	

Does participant have seizures? Yes___No___If yes, what type (grand mal, petit mal, other, please describe)

Please provide specfic information for any medical conditions we should be aware of (allergies, etc.).

Please list any prohibited activities or precautions.

Please identify type, dosage, and time of all medication participant is currently taking.

MEDICATION: Type   Dosage   Time

_____

_____

_____

CONFIDENTIALITY RELEASE

I, the undersigned, hereby authorize the Cincinnati Recreation Commission to utilize photographs, video-tapes, or voice recordings of the participant to be used for research, education, and promotion of Recreation Commission programs.

_____
                     Signature of parent/guardian   Date

I, the undersigned, hereby authorize the Cincinnati Recreation Commission to contact school/work activity center concerning participant information that pertains to the recreation program.

_____
                     Signature of parent/guardian   Date

Continued

IV. SWIMMING

Please identify (check) the participant's swim skill level:
Nonswimmer___Beginner___Intermediate___Advanced___

Please explain the swim skills he/she can perform (face in water, front float, back float, etc.):

Please identify any special swimming precautions:

V. PROGRAM INFORMATION

Please identify participant's interests and activities previously enjoyed:

Please identify participant's dislikes and/or inappropriate activities:

Please identify behavior management techniques and/or effective behavior reinforcers:

Please identify areas for development and goals for instruction:

Please provide any additional information that may assist us with program delivery:

Continued

As a participant or parent/guardian of the participant in this program, I recognize that there are certain risks of physical injury and I agree to assume the full risk of any injuries, damages, or loss which may be sustained as a result of participating in any and all activities connected with or associated with such program.

I agree to waive and relinquish all claims I may have, as a result of my or my son/daughter's participation in the program, against the Public Recreation Commission, City of Cincinnati, and their agents, employees, and volunteers.

I do hereby fully release and discharge the Public Recreation Commission, City of Cincinnati and their agents, employees, and volunteers for any and all claims from injuries, damage, or loss which I may have or which may accrue to me on account of my or my son/daughter's participation in the program.

I further agree to protect, defend, and hold harmless the Public Recreation Commission, City of Cincinnati and their agents, employees, and volunteers from any and all claims resulting from injuries, damages, and losses sustained by myself or my son/daughter or arising out of, connected with, or in any way associated with the activities of the program.

I have read and fully understand this release form. Before registration in this program is valid, this release form must be signed by participant or the participant's parent or legal guardian.

Signature of Participant/Parent/Guardian _____

Date _____

Swim Program:
Cincinnati Recreation Commission
DIVISION OF THERAPEUTIC RECREATION
Two Centennial Plaza, 805 Central Ave.
Cincinnati, OH 45202

SWIM REGISTRATION FORM
PARTICIPANT INFORMATION

Name_____ Male____ Female____ Birth date_____
     Last   First

Address_____Home phone_____
       Street   City   Zip

Parent/Guardian_____Work phone_____

School_____ Teacher_____

Please list a relative or friend to contact if parent/guardian cannot be reached:

Name_____ Phone_____

Physician_____ Phone_____

MEDICAL INFORMATION

Disabling condition_____

Medication: name/type_____

When taken:_____ Side effects, if any:_____

Is participant subject to seizures? Yes___ No___

If yes, what type:_____ Date of last seizure_____

How often does participant have seizures?_____

Is participant ambulatory? Yes___ No___

Does he/she walk with assistance? Yes___ No___

Does participant use a: Wheelchair___ Braces___ Crutches___

Please give any directions for proper use of ambulation equipment:

Continued

MEDICAL INFORMATION (*continued*)

Does participant have a heart condition? Yes___ No___

If yes, plesase specify any precautions:_____

Does participant have asthma? Yes___ No___

If yes, please specify any precautions:_____

Is participant a hepatitis carrier? Yes___ No___

Does participant have any speech impairment? Yes___ No___

If yes, to what degree?_____

Does participant have any hearing impairment? Yes___ No___

If yes, to what degree?_____

Does participant have tubes in ears? Yes___ No___
If yes, right ear ___ left ear ___

Does participant have molds for swimming? Yes___ No___
Ear plugs ___ Bathing cap___

Does participant have a visual impairment? Yes___ No___

If yes, to what degree?_____

Does participant dress himself/herself? Yes___ No___

If no, is assistance required? Total assistance___ Partial assistance___

Has the participant been swimming before? Yes___ No___

If yes, where?_____

Please explain the swimming skills he/she can perform (face in water, front float, back float, etc.):

Please list any special precautions:

Additional information which would help us in working with the participant:

Continued

PARTICIPANT/PARENT/GUARDIAN RELEASE

As a participant or parent/guardian of the participant in this program, I recognize that there are certain risks of physical injury and I agree to assume the full risk of any injuries, damages, or loss which may be sustained as a result of participating in any and all activities connected with or associated with such program.

I agree to waive and relinquish all claims I may have, as a result of my or my son/daughter's participation in the program, against the Public Recreation Commission, City of Cincinnati, and their agents, employees, and volunteers.

I do hereby fully release and discharge the Public Recreation Commission, City of Cincinnati and their agents, employees, and volunteers for any and all claims from injuries, damage, or loss which I may have or which may accrue to me on account of my or my son/daughter's participation in the program.

I further agree to protect, defend, and hold harmless the Public Recreation Commission, City of Cincinnati and their agents, employees, and volunteers from any and all claims resulting from injuries, damages, and losses sustained by myself or my son/daughter or arising out of, connected with, or in any way associated with the activities of the program.

I have read and fully understand this release form. Before registration in this program is valid, this release form must be signed by participant or the participant's parent or legal guardian.

Signature of Participant/Parent/Guardian ——————————————————————

Date ———————————————————

I am specifically granting permission to you to use likeness, voice, and words of the applicant in publicity, research, and education related to Cincinnati Recreation Commission programs.

SIGNATURE OF SELF (IF 13 YEARS OF AGE OR OLDER), PARENT, OR GUARDIAN

————————————————————————   ——————————————————

Signature of Participant/Parent/Guardian   Date

```
┌─────────────────────────────┐
│  AQUATICS MARY              ││   AM17              Reg.Date-08/09/93
└─────────────────────────────┘
```

Address ====> Cincinnati, OH
Parent/Grd.=>

MR	PD	LD	BD	AR	MI	Photo	MedWaiver
	Y					Y	Y

Birthdate ==> 08/23/74
Gender =====> F   Group Home ====>
Home Phone# > 1-800-POOL G.H. Contact ==>
Mom Work# ==>   School/Work ===>
Dad Work# ==>   Teacher/Supv.==>
Emergency# => 1-800-SWIM
Comments ===>

Doctor ======>
Med.Comments=> MUSCULAR DYSTROPHY, TRACHEOTOMY, VENTILATOR, USES "TRACH" PLUG WHILE IN WATER,
               SEIZURES. AVOID SPLASHING.

Medication	Dosage	Time(s)
PHENOBARBITAL	15MG	AM&PM

PERFORMANCE AREA *	* 1	2	3	4	5	6	7	8	9	10	11	12	13	14	15	16	17	18	19	20	21	22
Aquatics																						
Aquatics-Adjustment																						
Aquatics-Breath Control																						
Aquatics-Buoyancy/Float.																						
Aquatics-Propulsion																						

Staff Comments: SWIM OBJECTIVE: DURING FALL INSTRUCTION IN LEVEL 1 CLASS, MARY WILL DEVELOP
                BACK FLOAT WITH SUPPORT ACCORDING TO THE SWIM PROGRESSION
                PROGRESS NOTE: AT THE END OF THE FALL SESSION, MARY FLOATS ON BACK BUT DOES
                NOT EXHIBIT TRUST WITH INSTRUCTOR. CONTINUE TO DEVELOP STROKE IN SMALL GROUP
                SITUATION WITH INTERMITTENT USE OF OXYGEN TANK.

* Date/Progress
  -Date of Session
  -Observed-Yes : Not Observed-No

Glossary

Activity Analysis A process that breaks down experiences to determine the types and number of cognitive, emotional, social, and motor behaviors required to perform an activity; these behaviors become the skills listed in the swim progression.

Acute Sudden onset of illness or disability, as with asthma, or an accident causing paralysis.

Adapted/Specialized Program A swim program in which instruction and interactions are modified to ensure skill acquisition and personal development. Water safety, learning to swim, and developing a leisure skill are primary objectives.

Addictions Chronic progressive disorders like eating and substance abuse that have physical and psycho-social impairments.

Adipose Tissue Body fat; persons with more body fat than muscle tissue float more easily and those with muscle and heavy bone structure float less well.

Ambulatory The ability to move with or without the assistance of either an orthopedic or prosthetic device.

Americans with Disabilities Act of 1990 (ADA) P.L. 101-336; a civil rights law to eliminate discrimination against individuals with disabilities in employment, public services, transportation, public accommodations, and telecommunication services.

Americans with Disabilities Act Accessibility Guidelines (ADAAG) for Buildings and Facilities Criteria to assess physical access to public and commercial facilities.

Amputation Absence or loss of a limb or portion thereof.

Architectural & Transportation Barriers Compliance Board The body that monitors the ADAAG regulations.

Arteriosclerosis A group of cardiac diseases including atherosclerosis characterized by hardening of the arteries.

Arthritis Inflammation of the joints causing movement limitations.

Atherosclerosis Progressive degeneration that narrows coronary arteries affecting blood circulation to heart.

Atlantoaxial Instability Weakness in ligaments between first two vertebrae in spinal column of individual with Down Syndrome that could limit swimming activities.

Auditory Pertains to hearing and sound sensation.

Aura A sensation preceding onset of a seizure, such as smelling an odor or seeing colors, that might be reported by the swimmer.

Autism A pervasive developmental disorder with impairments in social interactions, communication, and imaginative activity.

Back Float Supine, face-up stationary water position.

Back Glide Moving through the water in a supine position.

Behavior Management Several strategies used to either increase or decrease participant behaviors by controlling the consequences of their displayed behaviors.

Bilateral Movement of both sides of the body; a breaststroke is a bilateral stroke.

Blind A person with less than 20/200 visual acuity in the better eye or less than a 20 degree field of vision after correction.

Bobbing Vertical jumping in the water with arm action pushing water upward then downward so the body submerges and resurfaces.

Buoyancy The ability of the body to float caused by an upward force of water on the body.

Catheter A tube used to withdraw urine from the bladder.

Center of Buoyancy Body rotates around this center when submerged; located in the chest area.

Center of Mass/Gravity Body weight is centered around this point located in the hip area.

Cerebral Palsy (CP) A nonprogressive lifelong physical disorder affecting movement caused by malfunction or damage to the brain.

Cerebral Vascular Accident/Stroke (CVA) Disorder caused by stoppage of blood circulation to part of the brain.

Chronic Long-term or recurring impact of illness or disability.

Colostomy Surgery creating an opening between large intestine and outside of the body to eliminate feces.

Congenital An illness or disability present since birth.

Contracture Shortening or reduction in muscle size caused by spasm, paralysis, disuse, or remaining in one position for a prolonged period of time.

Critical Incident Report A form used to note factors that could lead to risk or safety issues with swimmers, staff, and/or resources.

Cyanosis A bluish color of the skin indicating lack of oxygen caused by a breathing difficulty.

Cystic Fibrosis (CF) A hereditary respiratory disorder affecting children's ability to breath properly.

Deaf A person who is unable with or without a hearing aid to process linguistic information.

Diabetes Mellitus A chronic metabolic disorder characterized by large amounts of sugar in the blood.

Drag Water resistance to body movement through it that creates a vacuum through which the swimmer is able to move more easily; the instructor remains in front of the swimmer to create this vacuum.

Emotional Impairments Several disorders characterized by dysfunction in affect, social relationships, thoughts, perceptions, and reality.

Epilepsy, Seizure, Convulsive Disorder A central nervous system disorder marked by transient periods of unconsciousness.

European Backstroke A bilateral backstroke with both arms raised out of the water simultaneously to complete the arm stroke.

Explosive Breathing A technique in which the participant inhales through the mouth/nose, holds the breath, exhales forcefully through the mouth/nose, and then immediately inhales.

Finning Short pushes of the hands against the water in the opposite direction of travel to aid the swimmer in maintaining a float or initial propulsion.

Formative Evaluation Occurs during the program and is used to make immediate adjustments; swimmer's performance is measured against the steps of the swim progression to determine proper level of instruction.

Gastrostomy (G) Tube A tube placed in the stomach to provide supplemental or total nutrition.

Glide Movement through the water without completing a stroke.

Gravitational Insecurity (Earthboundness) Reluctance to leave vertical position, for example, to jump, lean, or climb up and down.

Hard-of-Hearing A person who is unable without a hearing aid to process linguistic information.

Hemiplegia Motor and sensory paralysis of one side or one half of the body as evident with a stroke or CVA.

Hepatitis B A contagious disease resulting in inflammation of the liver that may remain dormant for extended time periods and is transmitted through contact with body fluids or blood; a swim instructor may become a carrier as a result of contact with a swimmer's urine or through infected scratches.

Hyperventilate Air is retained in the lungs by limiting the number of exhalations; may cause a swimmer to become light-headed.

Ileostomy Surgery creating an opening between the small intestine and outside of the body to eliminate feces.

Incontinence Loss of the ability to control the bladder, bowel, or both.

Inverted Breathing An inhalation through the mouth with exhalation through the nose.

Inverted "C" Position Body position in the water on the back with the upper torso arched and lower torso curved in a semi-vertical position so body shape appears as an inverted "C."

Lateral Away from the body midline; with reference to a swim stroke, one that is completed one side at a time as with the crawl.

Learning Disability A specific developmental disorder resulting in inadequate development in language, speech, motor skills, and specific academic subjects like math or writing.

Lesion Discontinuation of tissue or loss of function of a part; the level of the lesion determines the remaining or residual degree of functioning.

Mainstream/Integrative Program A swim program in which swimmers receive individual and/or group instruction with others not identified as having an illness or disability and in which the focus is on not only acquisition of swim skills but also peer interactions and public behaviors.

Mental Retardation (MR) Lifelong cognitive impairment evident with subaverage intelligence and limitations in self care or activities of daily living (ADL).

Multiple Sclerosis (MS) A neurological disorder characterized by periods of exaggeration and remission with progressive degeneration affecting motor, sensory, communication, and cognitive functioning.

Muscular Dystrophies (MD) A progressive disorder resulting in muscle weakness and movement limitations.

Myocardial Infarction (MI) A heart attack.

National Council for Therapeutic Recreation Certification, Inc. (NCTRC) The body that certifies practitioners as Certified Therapeutic Recreation Specialists (CTRS) and provides study materials for their national competency examination; the organization of the disabilities in this manual is reflective of these study materials.

Nasogastric (NG) Tube A tube placed through the nose and down into the stomach for medications and nutrition.

Nonambulatory Requiring use of either electric and/or nonelectric wheelchair or motorized device to assist in movement.

Orthopedic Device An artificial device supporting the body or a body part like a walker or leg brace.

Paralysis Loss of sensation, voluntary motion, or both.

Paraplegia Lesion of the spinal cord at or below second thoracic vertebra (T2) resulting in either complete or incomplete loss of sensation and movement in both legs and the lower trunk.

Partially Sighted A person with at least 20/200 but less than 20/70 visual acuity in the better eye after correction.

Personal Floatation Device (PFD) Formerly a life jacket, graded by the amount of buoyancy provided, with Type I the most buoyant. Now includes a variety of devices to provide buoyancy.

Plan of Supervision A protocol or risk management document that specifies the recommended policies and procedures to manage a swim class.

Prone Face down position.

Prone Float Stationary face down position in the water.

Prone Glide Movement through the water in a prone position without completing a stroke.

Propulsion Motion or movement through the water by completing strokes.

Prosthesis Artificial or substitute limb or body part like an arm or eye.

Quadriplegia Lesion of the spinal cord above second thoracic vertebra (T2) resulting in either complete or incomplete loss of sensation and movement in all four limbs and body functions at or below the lesion level.

Range of Motion (ROM) Exercises or activities to increase the degree of movement of the muscles around the joints.

Risk Management Documented procedures to ensure safety and reduce risks in the aquatic environment.

Recovery Reference to the phase of the stroke when the arms and/or legs return to the initial or starting position and do not apply force on the water. Recovery may also refer to returning to vertical from horizontal position.

Scoliosis A curvature of the spine as seen with muscular dystrophies.

Sculling Movement of the hands at the side to propel the body through the water in a back float position.

Severe Multiple Impairment The person experiences one or more physical, cognitive, emotional, and/or social impairments that result in the need for lifelong assistance.

Social Impairments A variety of impairments, such as communicable diseases, sexually transmitted diseases (STDs), and crime that affect one's ability to manage personal life and social relationships.

Spina Bifida Several degrees of spinal cord defect noted at birth that can result in loss of sensation, bowel and bladder control, and limb control from lesion level downward.

Spinal Cord Injury (SCI) Damage to vertebrae of the spine accompanied by paralysis with location and extent of damage determining degree of paralysis and sensation loss.

Summative Evaluation Occurs after swim participation or program completion with information used to revise the individual's program plan, instructional variables, and variables in the aquatic setting.

Supine Face up position, as with the back float.

Swim Progression Sequence of skills to be performed; the progression is organized into four skill areas — adjustment to the aquatic environment, breath control, buoyancy and floatation, and propulsion leading to basic swim strokes.

Tactile Pertains to touch and discrimination of pressure.

Task Analysis A process that results in a sequence listing from first to last the skills necessary to perform a task, such as a swim stroke.

Therapeutic Program A swim program in which the focus is on functional skill improvement as prescribed by the treatment or rehabilitation plan.

Traumatic A sudden bodily injury with the potential of having a lasting or lifelong impact.

Traumatic Brain Injury (TBI) An insult to the brain by an external force that produces an altered level of consciousness and temporary or permanent impairment of functioning.

Associations

American Alliance for Health, Physical Education, Recreation and Dance, 1900 Association Drive, Reston, VA 22091

American Canoe Association, Disabled Paddlers Committee, 8580 Cinderbed Road, Ste. 1900, P.O. Box 1190, Newington, VA 22122-1190

American Red Cross, National Headquarters, 431 18th Street, NW, Washington, DC 20006

American Therapeutic Recreation Association, P.O. Box 15215, Hattiesburg, MS 39404-5215

American Water Ski Association, Disabled Ski Committee, Adaptive Aquatics, Inc., P.O. Box 7, Morven, GA 31638

Aquatic Exercise Association, 1032 S. Spring, P.O. Box 497, Port Washington, WI 53074

Arjo-century, Inc., 6380 Oakton Street, Morton Grove, IL 60053

Arthritis Foundation National Office, 1314 Spring Street, NW, Atlanta, GA 30309

Council for National Cooperation in Aquatics (CNCA), 901 W. New York Street, Indianapolis, IN 46202

Handicapped Scuba Association, 1104 El Prado, San Clemente, CA 92672

National Multiple Sclerosis Society, 733 3rd Avenue, New York, NY 10017

National Recreation and Park Association, Aquatic Section, 2775 S. Quincy Street, Ste. 300, Arlington, VA 22206-2204

Physically Challenged Swimmers of America, 22 William Street, #225, South Glastonbury, CT 06073

President's Council on Physical Fitness & Sports, The Presidential Fitness Mile Lap Swim for Special Populations, 450 Fifth Street, NW, Washington, DC 20001

Special Olympics International, 1350 New York Avenue, NW, Ste. 500, Washington, DC 20005-4709

U.S. Rowing Association, Adaptive Coordinator, 201 S. Capitol Avenue, Ste. 400, Indianapolis, IN 46225

U.S. Water Fitness Association, P.O. Box 3279, Boynton Beach, FL 33424-3279

YMCA of the USA, 14th Floor, 101 N. Wacker Drive, Chicago, Il 60606

YWCA of the USA, 726 Broadway, New York, NY 10003

Bibliography

Adams, R. C., & McCubbin, J. A. (1991). *Games, sports, and exercises for the physically disabled* (4th ed.). Philadelphia: Lea & Febiger.

American National Red Cross. (1992). *American Red Cross swimming & diving*. St. Louis, MO: Mosby-Year Book, Inc.

American National Red Cross. (1992). *American Red Cross water safety instructor's manual*. St. Louis, MO: Mosby-Year Book, Inc.

Aquatics International. Communication Channels, Inc., P.O. Box 1147, Skokie, Il 60076-9739.

Arthritis Foundation and the National Council of the Young Men's Christian Association of the USA. (1990). *Arthritis Foundation YMCA aquatic program (AFYAP) and AFYAP plus guidelines and procedures* (2nd ed.). Atlanta, GA: Authors.

Carter, M. J., Browne, B., LeConey, S. P., & Nagle, C. J. (1991). *Designing therapeutic recreation programs in the community*. Reston, VA: AALR/AAHPERD.

Crawford, M. E., & Mendell, R. (1987). *Therapeutic recreation and adapted physical activities for mentally retarded individuals*. Englewood Cliffs, NJ: Prentice-Hall, Inc.

Dunn, J. M., & Fait, H. F. (1989). *Special physical education: Adapted, individualized, developmental* (6th ed.). Dubuque, IA: Wm. C. Brown Publishers.

Horvat, M. (1990). *Physical education and sport for exceptional students*. Dubuque, IA: Wm. C. Brown Publishers.

Martin, J. (1981). The Halliwick method. *Physiotherapy*, 67(10), 288-291.

McGovern, J. (1992). *The ADA self-evaluation, a handbook for compliance with the Americans with Disabilities Act by parks and recreation agencies*. Arlington, VA: National Recreation and Parks Association.

Palaestra. P.O. Box 508, Macomb, IL 61455.

Rehabilitation literature. National Easter Seal Society, 2023 W. Ogden Avenue, Chicago, IL 60612.

Sherrill, C. (1993). *Adapted physical activity, recreation and sport: Cross-disciplinary and lifespan* (4th ed.). Madison, WI: WCB Brown & Benchmark Publishers.

Sports'n Spokes. Paralyzed Veterans of America, Inc., 2111 E. Highland, Ste. 180, Phoenix, AZ 85016-4702

Thomas, D. G. (1989). *Swimming steps to success*. Champaign, IL: Leisure Press.

United States Swimming, Adapted Swimming Committee. (1989). *Handbook for adapted competitive swimming* (3rd ed.). Libby Anderson.

YMCA of the USA. (1987). *Aquatics for special populations*. Champaign, IL: Human Kinetics Publishers, Inc.

Index

NOTES

NOTES

NOTES

NOTES